*Home Sweet Home Page*

DISCARD

# Home Sweet Home Page

**Robin Williams**
**Dave Mark**

Peachpit Press
Berkeley • California

# Home Sweet Home Page

**Robin Williams, with Dave Mark**
Illustrated by John Tollett

**Peachpit Press**   2414 Sixth Street
Berkeley, California 94710
510.548.4393 phone
510.548.5991 fax
Find Peachpit Press on the World Wide Web at **http://www.peachpit.com**
Find the Home Sweet Home Page web site
   at **http://www.peachpit.com/home-sweet-home**

Peachpit Press is a division of Addison Wesley Longman

Copyright ©1996 **Robin Williams** and **Dave Mark**
Cover illustration and cover design by **John Tollett**
Interior illustrations by **John Tollett**
Interior design and production by **Robin Williams**
Editing and proofreading by **Jenifer Blakemore**
Peachpit Press editing, proofreading, and production by **Nancy Davis** and **Kate Reber**

**ISBN**   0-201-88667-7

9 8 7 6 5 4 3 2 1
Printed and bound in the United States of America

## To my family:

the Williamses, the Webers,
the Nelsons, the Gardners,
some of whom I have lost touch with.
May we all meet together again,
across time and space.
However we connect,
whether in person,
by mail, telephone, fax,
or electronically,
it is real.
We are family.

*Robin*

And a special dedication
to Floyd Williams—
Uncle Floyd, I miss you. This book was for you.
R.

## To Deneen, Daniel, and Kelley:

Thanks for all you've given me.
LFUEMISF,OK?

*Dave*

# Thanks

We want to thank David Rogelberg of Studio B for the original concept for this book, and for choosing us as the ones to pull it off. We do hope it's what you had in mind, David!

And so many thanks to Ted Nace, publisher of Peachpit Press, for his continued support and wise guidance; Jenifer Blakemore for her editing, proofreading, and oh-so-thoughtful suggestions; Nancy Davis for patiently hanging in there, massaging and guiding the production of the book, and for our delightful conversational interludes; Kate Reber for her expert technical production eye; John Tollett for the beautiful illustrations that add so much to the appearance of the book, and for all the late-night graphic help squeezed between his own deadlines; our kids for their patience (do they have a choice? Scarlett says, "You're *always* almost finished with the book, Mom."). It's true that "The first half of any book takes 90 percent of the alloted time; the second half takes the other 90 percent."

*rw + dm*

Your attitude is your life.

# Contents

**PART II**

# Before and After

**PART III**     *Get Ready, Get Set*

A stone, a leaf,
an unfound door . . .
And all of the forgotten faces.

**Look Homeward, Angel**
~Thomas Wolfe

# Introduction

I just returned from a wonderful family reunion in a small town in Arkansas; there my belief was reinforced that even families that begin in small towns become fragmented—its members scattering across the country. This is not a new trend—this has been a way of life since the Pilgrims landed in America. Another part of our American history is immigration, which means many of us have family in other parts of the world.

Long ago, if you wanted to visit with your relatives in another town (let alone another country), it was a difficult journey—the farther away, the more difficult. Even sending a letter took a very long time. Then staying in touch got easier with trains, cars, and planes. The telephone made it possible to communicate when you couldn't actually be there in person. Mail got faster until it started appearing overnight, and fax machines don't even take that long. E-mail is even easier than faxing. Now with the Internet, we can connect and communicate in so many different ways, and it's fun. It's rich. It's empowering. The traditional boundaries of time and space are disappearing. Since it is a plain fact that generations of our families no longer live in the same village, here at last is a new technology that provides an opportunity for all of us, everywhere, to connect and stay in touch, using one central location, one global "refrigerator door" upon which to post messages, announcements, and news that everyone in the family, no matter where they are in the world, can access at any time.

> *Even a small family is large and contains multitudes.*
>
> Robin Williams, paraphrasing Walt Whitman

*They are your Family.*
*Love them*
*even if you*
*don't like them.*
*Stick together.*
*Families are the*
*Stuff of Life.*

Family is important. Family is all we've got. It doesn't matter that you don't get along all the time. You are family. It breaks my heart to hear of parents who disown their daughters because they got pregnant, their sons because they are gay, or of siblings who don't speak to each other. I was lucky. I was raised in a family devoted to unconditional love. I credit much of my success in life to this great gift: the solid bond of family. Whether or not you were fortunate enough to have that as you were growing up, you can choose to create it and give it back to the world, to your own family. You begin with communicating; communicating is connecting.

The World Wide Web is the most exciting and powerful means of communication to occur on earth. Its effect on our society will be profound, bigger than the telephone, greater than the television. This book teaches you how to use this technology to connect with your entire family and all of your friends. This book encourages everyone to communicate, wherever they may be. I guarantee that in the **process** you will discover things about each other; you will find surprising depths in relatives you don't even know; you will establish, maintain, and strengthen bonds.

*The process*
*is just as important*
*as the product.*

Never before have the limitations of time and space been so easily bridged, and with so much potential. We are making history right now, and it's our job to use this technology for good things. Family is a good thing.

*with love, and I'll see you online,*
*Robin*

# Part One

# What's it All About?

in which we explain the basics of e-mail,
the Internet, and the World Wide Web,
and help you get comfortable
with this exciting new means
of communication.

**Browser**

Erma Bombeck said, "I found a letter to my sister the other day that I had forgotten to mail. It just needed a little updating to send. After 'the baby is . . .' I crossed out 'toilet trained' and wrote in 'graduating from high school this month.'"

# Chapter One
# E-Mail

This book is about computers. It's about family and friends. But mostly, this book is about keeping in touch. As you make your way through these pages, you'll learn about an amazing technology that was born only a few years ago, yet has dramatically changed the way people communicate. This technology is known as the World Wide Web, and it belongs to you.

We'll start off with an introduction to **e-mail** and the **Internet**, the vast collection of computers and phone lines that brings all of our computers together.

http://www.peachpit.com/home-sweet-home

# Keeping in Touch

There are many advantages that come with owning a computer. You can run your small business, do your taxes, even play your favorite game. But there's something much more important that your computer can help you do, and that's keep in touch with your friends and family.

In the early days, the best way to keep in touch was by post. You either lived close to the folks you cared about or you wrote them letters. Then, a remarkable invention revolutionized the way people communicated. This invention formed an intricate network, connecting to every home in the country and, eventually, spread throughout the world. Of course, this invention was the telephone.

The telephone definitely made it easier to keep in touch. But the best was still to come. In the middle of the twentieth century, a scientist at Bell Laboratories invented the transistor. The transistor paved the way for the invention of the computer, and the computer and the telephone turned out to be an incredible combination.

# Computers and telephones

They've changed the way we live. Remember your first answering machine? Someone could actually leave you a message even if you weren't home. And how about the fax machine? Sure, with a telephone you could send a voice message, but with a fax machine you could send a written message, a picture or photograph, or even a 100-page business proposal complete with charts and graphics. Seriously cool!

Now things are really getting interesting. Suddenly, many people have personal computers in their homes. Chances are, since you are reading this book, you've got a computer at home, too. And the wonderful thing is, using a **modem**, you can hook your computer and your telephone together. You plug the modem into your computer, then plug your modem into the phone jack in the wall (or you may have a computer with a modem built right in).

**modem**: *a little device attached to or built inside your computer. You see, the phone lines right now can only understand "analog" information. Analog stuff is like water—infinite, flowing. But the computer can only understand "digital" information—finite, absolute, countable, like ice cubes.*

Once you've got your computer connected to your phone line, your computer can communicate with any other computer that is also connected to a phone line. If you have a cousin in Denmark with a computer and a modem, your computer can communicate with your cousin's computer. If you can reach someone by phone, your computers can communicate.

*So the computer sends ice cubes (digital info) to your modem.*

*Your modem turns the ice cubes into water (analog info) and sends it through the phone lines.*

*The modem on the other computer turns the analog info (water) back into the exact same digital info (ice cubes) it started out as so the other computer can understand it.*

## Sending electronic mail

So why would you want your computer to communicate with someone else's computer? One of the best reasons is so you can send and receive **electronic mail**—affectionately known as **e-mail**.

Suppose you wanted to put together a family recipe book, gathering recipes from all of your relatives to preserve them for future generations. You could send out letters to all your relatives, then wait a week or so for their replies to get back to you. You've then got to type all those recipes into your computer. Boring.

With e-mail, your job is so much easier. Type a quick message asking folks for their recipes, then e-mail the letter to all of your relatives (of course, you'll have to convince all your relatives to get e-mail as well, but once you've spent some time communicating this way, you'll have no problem convincing others to do the same). Your letter will arrive in their electronic mailboxes within seconds. Then they'll send e-mail back to you with their favorite recipes. If your timing is right, you might get a reply within minutes!

As these recipes come back to you, you'll copy the text from the e-mail and paste it directly into your electronic family recipe book without having to retype a word. Electronic mail means no paper to waste, no stamps to lick, and no waiting for someone to lug your letters around the country. E-mail is environmentally friendly and e-mail is fast.

# How e-mail works

Sending e-mail is a lot like making a telephone call.

On a **local phone call**, your call goes to your local phone company, zips through some switches, then heads out to the person you are calling.

 *A local phone call*

On a **long-distance call**, your call goes to the local phone company, gets routed through your long distance company, then on to the local phone company of the person you are calling.

 *A long-distance phone call*

When you send **e-mail**, the message goes through a similar process:

Your e-mail goes to a computer owned by your e-mail service provider. If your message is addressed to **someone who subscribes to the same e-mail service**, the message goes straight to that person's mailbox where it sits waiting for them to check their mail.

 *A "local" e-mail message*

If your e-mail is addressed to **someone on a different e-mail service**, the e-mail must go through a "gateway" between your e-mail provider and your friend's e-mail provider.

 *A "long-distance" e-mail message*

## An e-mail example

So, to further explain that last example, suppose you subscribe to America Online (an extremely popular service that provides e-mail as one of its benefits) and your cousin Lew subscribes to Compu-Serve (another popular service). When you send an e-mail to Lew, it goes from your computer to a computer in one of America Online's buildings.

If your message is sent to someone else on America Online (a local call), it is placed in that person's mailbox on the America Online computer, waiting for that person to check their mail.

But since Cousin Lew subscribes to CompuServe, your message needs to travel over the "long-distance lines" between America Online and CompuServe, through the gateway, also known as the **Internet**. Once your message arrives at CompuServe, it gets placed into Cousin Lew's mailbox.

*So your mail goes from your computer to America Online.*

*It goes through the Internet (represented by these fat cables).*

*It goes to the computers at CompuServe, where Lew can pick it up.*

We'll explain more about e-mail in the next chapter, but first a word about the Internet itself.

# Chapter Two
# The Internet

You've seen one important way that computers can help you keep in touch with your friends and family: electronic mail. E-mail lets you send a message from your computer to someone else's computer, without using a single sheet of paper, without having to find an envelope and a stamp and the correct street address, and without having to take the letter down to the post office.

In this chapter, you're going to learn more about the technology that makes this computer-to-computer communication possible: the

## Internet.

# What is the Internet?

Any electronic mail service (online service) worth its salt will offer you a connection to the Internet. America Online, CompuServe, Prodigy, and the Microsoft Network all offer Internet access. But what does that mean?

You already know that the Internet lets you pass messages between different electronic mail services. But what, exactly, is the Internet?

The Internet consists of a specific set of computers, along with all the computers connected, no matter how remotely, to those computers. This means that if you connect your computer to the Internet, *you* become part of the Internet.

Some of the specific computers that make up the Internet belong to colleges and universities. Some belong to the military and some to the government. Some belong to private industry. The vast majority of these computers offer electronic mail. Anyone connected to any of these computers can send e-mail to anyone else connected to any of these computers. One way to look at the Internet is as a great big electronic mail service. But the Internet is much more than that.

# More than just e-mail

The Internet offers a fantastic range of services, from e-mail to file transfer, from mailing lists to our favorite service of all, the World Wide Web.

## Transferring files

Using the Internet, you can **transfer files** from your computer to someone else's and from another computer to yours. This means you can send a spreadsheet to your tax preparer or obtain a set of plans for that tree house you've always wanted to build.

## Newsgroups

The Internet also offers a service known as **newsgroups**. A newsgroup is a collection of messages relating to a specific topic. For example, the newsgroup known as *sci.med.nutrition* is filled with messages all related to nutrition. Some of the messages are from nutritional experts, looking for the latest information or comparing notes with their colleagues. Some are from people looking for advice. Most newsgroups are run like a community. The expert users help the novices. If you don't know, ask (after you've read the **FAQ**!). Once you become an expert, you help the other folks.

There are thousands of newsgroups, covering topics like childcare, quilting, baseball, classical music—you name it. Using a "newsgroup reader" (most online services and service providers offer them) you can look through the list of available newsgroups and subscribe to the ones that interest you. Once you are subscribed to a newsgroup, you can scan the messages posted by other folks, or you can post some messages of your own.

Newsgroups are a great way to keep up on your favorite subject and a great way to get those difficult questions answered.

**FAQ:** *Frequently Asked Questions. You will often see references to or you will come across actual files of FAQs. These are lists of the most common questions regarding any newsgroup or software product, etc. Before asking questions or poking your nose into a newsgroup, it is mandatory that you read their FAQ.*

## Mailing lists (listservs)

Similar to a newsgroup, a **listserv** is a subscription mailing list dedicated to a specific topic. Once you subscribe to a listserv, you get every message sent to anyone else on the list, showing up in your box as e-mail. There are thousands of lists on a variety of topics.

Listservs can be cool, but they can also take a lot of your time. Once you find a listserv you want to subscribe to, be sure to find out how to "unsubscribe" in case you change your mind and want to stop the flood of e-mail messages into your mail box. Most listservs tell you how to unsubscribe at the same time as they tell you how to subscribe. Save that information!

## And more

The Internet lets you use your computer to listen to long-distance **radio** or **television** programs and even make inexpensive **long-distance telephone calls**. There are boatloads of existing Internet services with more and more appearing online all the time.

## World Wide Web

Most importantly, the Internet gives you access to the **World Wide Web**, affectionately known as **the web**. The web mixes text, graphics, sound, e-mail, and file transfer all under a single umbrella.

The web is what *Home Sweet Home Page* is all about. By the time you finish this book, you'll know how to make your way around the web, and you'll also know how to create your own web site.

Before you can take advantage of any of the Internet services, you first have to get connected to the Internet.

# Accessing the Internet

To connect your computer to the Internet, you've got two basic choices. You can subscribe to an **online service** such as America Online, CompuServe, Prodigy, or the Microsoft Network, or you can sign up with an **Internet service provider (ISP)**. First let's take a look at the advantages and disadvantages of connecting to the Internet using an online service.

## Online services

An online service is like a combination town hall and community library, filled with useful information and friendly, helpful people. America Online is easily the most popular online service in the world, with more than five million people connected.

Online services such as America Online and CompuServe offer a wide range of services, including e-mail and access to the Internet. The **advantage** to using an online service for your Internet access is that online services tend to be very easy to use. For example, the illustration below shows the services offered by America Online. To take a look at the day's news highlights, just click on the button labeled "Today's News." To access the Internet, click on the button labeled "Internet Connection." It couldn't be easier.

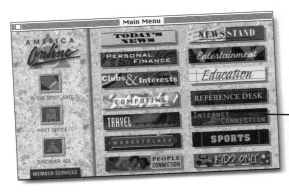

*This is the "Internet Connection" button on the welcome window of America Online*

There is a **disadvantage** to using an online service for your Internet access. Online services tend to "bury" their Internet access beneath layers of buttons and windows. While this makes it easier to learn how to use each service, the extra layers tend to make using the Internet a little less efficient and a little more work. You'll see this yourself as you start to use the Internet.

**speed**: *how fast information can travel from one computer to another. The speed is measured in* **bits per second (bps)**, *which many people think is the same as the* **baud rate**. *They are not the same, but we're not going to worry about the technical differences. Just know that when you hear people speak in numbers, they are talking about how fast information travels.*

*2400 baud used to be fast; now it's considered slow. To be on the Internet you really should have a modem with a speed of at least 14.4 (shorthand for 14,400, pronounced "fourteen four"), and preferably 28.8 (28,800, pronounced "twenty-eight eight"). It won't be long before 28.8 is "slow."*

Also, in some areas the **speed** of access is limited for online services, no matter how fast your modem is. For instance, in Santa Fe the speed for America Online has been only 2400, which is phenomenally slow. To use the Internet at 2400 is dreadfully frustrating and deadly dull. With a fast modem and a direct connection with an Internet service provider, you can browse the Internet at speeds of at least 28,800 (called 28.8).

## Internet Service Providers

If you plan on spending a lot of time on the Internet, or if you don't need the extra features offered by the online services, consider signing up with an Internet service provider (ISP). An Internet service provider is a company that provides direct, high-speed access to the Internet.

You see, when you sign on to an online service such as America Online, you'll run the software provided by them. This software is an all-in-one package, wrapping everything you need to access the service in a single application. Typically, online service software is very nicely designed, easy to use, and, most importantly, very consistent. For example, the window that lists all your e-mail messages looks much like the window that lists all of today's news or the latest sports scores. This consistency is a real advantage, especially if you're new to the service.

⌂ http://www.peachpit.com/home-sweet-home

Unfortunately, this consistency breaks down when it comes to accessing the **Internet**. The major online services were built before the Internet and the World Wide Web gained their current popularity. Basically, the online services were just not built to work with the Internet, and it shows. (However, as we speak, the folks at CompuServe are moving their entire service to the Internet.)

But when you sign up with an Internet service provider, you'll get a *bunch* of software utilities and applications instead of the single, integrated package that comes with your online service. For starters, you'll get some software that allows you to communicate over the Internet. Depending on your computer configuration, this software can be difficult to install—most people need help. Ask for it.

Once you get connected to the Internet, you'll have some choices to make. You can use an all-in-one package like Netscape Navigator to send files, access the World Wide Web, send and receive e-mail, and participate in Internet newsgroups.

(While an integrated package like Netscape Navigator does an adequate job, many users prefer a more separated approach. They might use Navigator to access the World Wide Web, plus software called NewsWatcher to access newsgroups, Anarchie for file transfer, and Eudora for e-mail. Once you are connected to the Internet, getting these Internet packages to work is usually pretty straightforward.)

The bottom line: you'll get better performance with an Internet service provider, but at the cost of a steeper learning curve. With an online service, you've got just one application to master. With an Internet service provider, you have to first get connected to the Internet, then master either an integrated package or a different application for each Internet service you want to use.

# Which to use: online service or ISP?

If you have never used the Internet before, we suggest you try one of the online services to begin with. They are so easy to set up and to use, especially if you are just learning the ropes. But they are also relatively expensive because they are doing so much of the work for you.

If you have been on the Internet and are already an active participant (or if you are planning to be), it behooves you to get a direct connection through an ISP so you can get the fastest speeds and the best performance.

Throughout the rest of this book, we're going to assume you have access to the Internet, either via an online service or an ISP. Be sure to check out the Home Sweet Home Page web site (the address is at the bottom of every page), which can direct you to service providers and other useful information and resources.

Right now, let's get a little more specific about e-mail.

# An e-mail address

Your online name (also called your "screen name") or your online "address" is how people will reach you. Suppose your America Online screen name is **jjones**. To other folks who are also subscribers on America Online, you'll be known as **jjones**. For example, if someone on America Online were to send you e-mail, they would address it to **jjones**.

If you have an account with CompuServe, your address is not an easily recognizable and memorable word, but a number such as 12345,6789. Although it looks different, it's the same thing as a screen name on America Online.

The important thing to remember is that no matter what the phrase looks like—a real name or a bunch of numbers—that phrase is your **address** to which mail is sent.

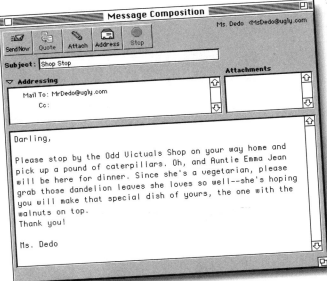

This is a typical e-mail form. Depending on which software you use, your form may look a little different. But you will always have a place to enter the address (here it says "Mail To"), a place to type your message, and almost always a Subject box to fill in.

The "Cc" stands for "carbon copy," a holdover from the days of carbon (remember those days?). You can type other addresses in the Cc area and those people will get this same message.

## Addressing to another service

One of the beauties of the Internet is that it connects us all together, no matter which service you are on. So someone with an account on CompuServe, Prodigy, or any other service that includes a connection to the Internet, can also send e-mail to jjones.

If you want to send e-mail to a service other than the one you are using, you'll need to add a little bit more to the address. For example, if you are on CompuServe and want to send e-mail to jjones at America Online, you'll address the e-mail to:

**jjones@aol.com**

This is pronounced "jjones at ay-oh-el dot com." The "@aol.com" part tells the e-mail software to send this e-mail to America Online (the service itself is often called "AOL"). Once the e-mail gets there, America Online will deliver it to jjones.

If you are on America Online and want to send e-mail to your friend on CompuServe, you must change the comma in their address to a period, and add CompuServe's name so it looks like this:

**12345.6789@compuserve.com**

When you want to communicate with someone via the Internet, it's not enough to give them your plain online name or address (in this case, "jjones" or "12345,6789"). You must always give them your complete "Internet" address (in this case "jjones@aol.com"). The part of your Internet address that comes after the "@" (pronounced "at") is known as a **domain name**.

# The domain name

The domain name is important. It tells the world what part of the Internet someone belongs to. America Online subscribers all have the domain name "aol.com," CompuServe uses "compuserve.com," Prodigy uses "prodigy.com," and Microsoft Network uses "msn.com." Each of these is a domain name. When you give someone your e-mail address, be sure to include the domain name!

In the US, all domain names end with either **.com**, **.edu**, **.gov**, **.mil**, **.net**, or **.org**. This part of the name gives you a clue as to where you are sending or receiving the mail:

**domain name**: *the period in the domain name is pronounced "dot." Thus "cornell.edu" is pronounced "cornell dot ee-dee-you." The name "prodigy.com" is pronounced "prodigy dot com." To type the dot, of course, you type a period.*

**.com** **com**mercial organizations (businesses, such as zumacafe.com)

**.edu** **edu**cational institutions (cornell.edu)

**.gov** **gov**ernment organizations (nasa.gov)

**.mil** **mil**itary organizations (army.mil)

**.net** **net**work organizations (internic.net)

**.org** **org**anizations that don't fit in any of the other categories, usually non-profits (for instance, software.org is the The Software Productivity Consortium, a nonprofit organization)

Domain names belonging to other countries always end in a two-character "country code." For example, the domain name "ox.ac.uk" belongs to Oxford University in Great Britain ("uk" stands for United Kingdom). Below is a list of country codes for various countries.

| | | | |
|---|---|---|---|
| **jp** | Japan | **au** | Australia |
| **ca** | Canada | **fr** | France |
| **de** | Germany | **mx** | Mexico |
| **ru** | Russia | **ch** | Switzerland |
| **us** | United States | **uk** | United Kingdom |

http://www.peachpit.com/home-sweet-home

Don't worry too much about the structure of a domain name. The important thing is to be able to pick one out of a crowd. When you see something like this:

**terryTiger@research.santafe.edu**

think **domain name!** In this case, the online name is "terryTiger" and the domain name is "research.santafe.edu." This address comes from the research lab at the Santa Fe Institute.

## E-mail address versus web address

The @ symbol (pronounced "at") is your clue that the address is for e-mail.

**robin@zumacafe.com** is an e-mail address

When you see an address with a domain name that does **not** have the @ symbol, it is a reference for a page or file somewhere on the Internet, but it is not e-mail!

**http://www.zumacafe.com** is **not** an e-mail address, but an address on the World Wide Web

## Next stop: the World Wide Web

Now that you have a bit of background on the Internet, it's time to get your fingers dirty. Yes, you are about to venture out onto the World Wide Web. And it'll be fun—I guarantee it.

# Chapter Three
# The World Wide Web

So far, we've seen the Internet as a vast network of computers, similar to the telephone network that allows you to call just about anyone else on the planet. If your computer is connected to the Internet, you are connected to every other computer connected to the Internet.

Another way to look at the Internet is as a vast, global, flea market. Just as you wander through a flea market, leisurely browsing the wares, you can also browse the Internet, searching for a specific piece of information, or just enjoying an interesting electronic stroll. The **World Wide Web** is what makes this possible.

http://www.peachpit.com/home-sweet-home

# Electronic publishing on the Web

Have you ever wanted to write a letter to the editor of a major newspaper? Have you ever wanted to publish your theory of crop circles, or the effect of television on the attention span of children? Imagine being able to publish anything you like, any time you like, and reaching a worldwide audience. Got a story to tell? Publish it on the web. Have a secret cache of recipes you are just aching to share? Publish it on the web. Want to share those pictures of your grandkids with the rest of us? Publish them on the web.

The World Wide Web is a vast collection of published information of all sorts. It is comprised of millions of individual **web pages** which you view one at a time. Large corporations, small businesses, families, individuals, schools, and so on can create their own collection of web pages relating to their particular interest. Each group of these pages of related information that someone creates is known as a **web site**. Each web site has a specific **web address**. To visit a web site, you'll use a piece of software known as a **web browser.**

Netscape Navigator is the most popular browser software in the world, but it is definitely not the only browser. Microsoft Explorer is another popular browser, as is NCSA Mosaic. Though there may be differences, in general a web site should look about the same no matter which browser you use.

And this is yet another browser, Browser Dawg.

⌂ http://www.peachpit.com/home-sweet-home

# Where do you get a web browser?

There are a number of web browsers out there. The most popular are Netscape Navigator and Microsoft's Internet Explorer.

Most likely, your Internet provider will give you a web browser when you sign up for your service. If not, you can buy a browser at most computer stores for less than $50. Or if you have a friend who's already on the Internet, ask them to download a browser for you. Also, at any bookstore you can find Internet books with enclosed disks that often include a free web browser.

# Visiting a web site

**To visit a web site**, first you'll connect to the Internet, then you'll open your web **browser** software. Finally, you'll type in the **address** of the web **site** you'd like to visit (details on page 42) and press the Return or Enter key.

As soon as you press Return or Enter, your web **browser** proceeds to find the web **site** whose **address** you specified. If your Internet connection is up and running, and if the web site you are trying to reach is up and running, the text and pictures stored on the first **page** of that web site will start to appear in your web browser's window. Let's look at each of these concepts in more detail.

There are all kinds of web sites out there, just waiting for you to find them. Let's walk through one—Robin's Ballyhoo.Inc site:

### http://www.ballyhoo-inc.com

This is the web address you can enter later, but for right now, just read on to get the idea.

Hey, they call me Url Ratz.

## Exploring a site

Once you enter the address for the Ballyhoo site and hit Return or Enter, your browser will take you to the page you see below, which is the **home page** for Ballyhoo.Inc:

home page: *The home page is generally considered to be the first page of a* **web site** *(the collection of individual pages). Some people only have one page in their web site, so their home page* **is** *the entire web site.*

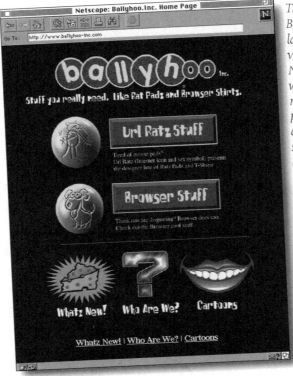

*This is what the Ballyhoo.Inc web site looks like when viewed using the Netscape Navigator web browser. The main area of the page is called the content area. (Web sites are constantly evolving–don't be surprised if it looks different the next time you go there!)*

While the text and graphics are nice to look at, they are only part of the **web site**. The site is made up of several individual **web pages**. (In fact, the entire World Wide Web is actually just millions of these individual pages, linked together.)

# Linking the pages together

So how do you move around to the other web pages in a site? By clicking on **links**. A link appears on a web page, and when you click on it, it takes you to another page *or* to somewhere else on the same page. We'll talk more about links and how to recognize them in a minute. To test one, (pretend to) click on the graphic image of the cheese, labeled "Whatz New!" on the preceding page. The web browser will jump to a page displaying the newest products in the Ballyhoo.Inc line.

*If you click on the "Whatz New!" cheese image on the Ballyhoo.Inc home page, you will jump to this display of what's new in the line.*

Take a look at the bottom of the web page shown above. Notice the graphics and the line of text that looks like this:

**Home Page** | **Who Are We?** | **Cartoons**

Each of the graphics is a link, and each of the underlined words also act as links to the same place (just in case you're using a web browser that doesn't show graphics). For example, if you click on the words Home Page, *or* if you click on the round Url button, your web browser will take you back to the Ballyhoo.Inc home page. On a web page, anything can act as a link.

## Finding the links

By convention, any text that is linked to something else is underlined. If you have a color monitor, text links are in color. Once you click on a link, its color changes. Once on the web, you will quickly notice there is a color indicating "You haven't clicked me yet" and another color indicating "You've already been there." That way, you can tell just by looking at a page how many links you have yet to follow.

On my color monitor, the Home Page text link on the Ballyhoo.Inc site is purple, while the Who Are We? and the Cartoons text links are bright blue. That's because I've already been to the Home Page, but I haven't yet *followed* (clicked on) the other links. Once you get used to using your software, you can choose the colors you want your links displayed in.

Text links are easy to spot since they are always underlined. Photographs, graphics, and other images can also act as links. The buttons of Url and Browser, the headlines, the little graphics, and the underlined text on the Ballyhoo.Inc home page all act as links.

*These three graphics are also links. If you click on any one of them, the browser will take you somewhere else, a separate page for each link.*

# Other visual clues for links

Since picture links aren't underlined, how do you tell which are links and which are just there to add to the look of the page? Sometimes a graphic will have a border around it, indicating it is a link to some-where else. The border will be the same color as the text links.

Also, most web browsers come with a built-in feature that helps you identify the various elements on a web page. In Netscape, when your mouse cursor passes over a link, the pointer turns into a little hand with a pointing finger. This is one clue that the item under the finger is a link—just click on it.

*When your pointer is positioned on top of a link, it turns into this little hand.*

Also, you'll notice that the web address associated with a link is displayed in the strip at the bottom of the browser window (see below). So another way to determine if a picture or word is a link is to position your pointer over it (don't click). If a web address appears in the strip at the bottom of the window, that item is a link to that web address (we'll talk more about web addresses in a minute). If this area remains blank and the pointer does not turn into a hand, the element you are pointing at is not a link.

Below you see how the web address appears in the address bar when you pass your pointer over the "Rat Padz" graphic.

*This is the address bar from the bottom of the Netscape browser window. Most browsers have a strip like this that displays the web address of the element your cursor points to.*

# Web addresses (URLs)

But my name is just Pronounced Url.

A **web address** is called a **URL** (pronounced "you are ell") which stands for Uniform Resource Locator (don't worry—you don't have to remember exactly what the letters stand for). Someone might say, "This is my URL." Or you might tell someone, "My URL is on my business card." On the facing page is an example of a URL for a web address, which is an address that will take you to a home page on the World Wide Web. There are other addresses that can take you to other places on the Internet besides the web, but we'll talk about those later in the book.

In most browsers there are several ways to enter a URL. In Netscape, for instance, one way is to go to the File menu, choose "Open Location…" (or press Command or Control L), type in the address, then click the "Open" button. Another way is to click the button called "Open" at the top of the Netscape screen, type in the address, then click "Open."

What most people do, though, is simply type the address into the **location box** (see below). The important thing to remember is that you must enter the entire address, including the "http://www." part. **After you type it in, you must hit the Enter or Return key to tell the browser to go get that page.** (If you're using Netscape, you don't need to type in the "http://" part; it will automatically appear after you hit the Enter key.)

This is the location box. Type the address in here. It's labeled "Go To" when you are typing in a new address, and "Location" once you are there.

# Anatomy of a web address

Below is an explanation of the various parts of a web address. You don't really have to know what they mean, but it's kind of interesting. All you really need to know is how to enter it into your browser.

*This part is sometimes called "blah blah blah" because it precedes almost every web page address.*

*You might think those are periods in the address below. They are, but in web and e-mail addresses they are pronounced "dot." So this part of the address is pronounced "www dot zumacafe dot com slash."*

## http://www.zumacafe.com/

*The "http" tells you* **this is a page on the World Wide Web**. *Other areas of the Internet have different prefixes. The prefix "news:" indicates a newsgroup (page 25). The prefix "ftp:" indicates a place where you can transfer files to your computer or sometimes read the text files (page 25).*

*The "www" is the standard indication for sites on the World Wide Web, but it is not always used. So don't assume an address is not a web page just because it uses something besides "www" here.*

*This is usually the name of the business that owns the web site. It's pretty clear who owns "disney.com," "toyota.com," or "apple.com." This is part of the domain name (see pages 32–34 for details).*

*The abbreviation ".com" tells you this site belongs to a* **com***mercial business. See page 33 for a list of the possible abbreviations you might see here and what they mean.*

## http://www.zumacafe.com/digiart.html

*Information after the domain name typically tells the browser to find another page in the same web site. This part may be quite long, as it might be deep inside folders and directories. See page 175 if you are curious about "html" files.*

# Wandering the web

Before you start to build your own web site, take some time (if you haven't already) to explore the web. The Home Sweet Home Page web site is a good place to start. There are links that will take you to other family sites, kids' sites, Mom or Dad sites, and just plain fun or interesting sites.

**bookmark:** *an electronic version of the traditional bookmark. It marks a web page for you so you can go to it instantly.*

You might want to make a **bookmark** for Home Sweet Home Page so you can always get there with just the click of a mouse:

⌂ In Netscape, while you are viewing the Home Sweet Home Page site, go to the Bookmarks menu and choose "Add Bookmark," or instead you can press Command D (Mac) or Control D (PC).

 *Choose this command while you are viewing the page you want to bookmark. The title of that page will then appear in the Bookmarks menu and you can select it at any time to jump to that page.*

⌂ Now whenever you want to go to the Home Sweet Home Page site, just choose its name from the Bookmarks menu.

This is the web address, the URL, for our site:

### http://www.peachpit.com/home-sweet-home

Notice the address is also at the bottom of every page of this book!

# Using a search engine

There are web sites on the Internet dedicated to helping you search for specific kinds of information. For example, there are sites that help you find people, sites that help you find jobs, sites that help you find other web sites. These helpful sites are known as **search engines**. If you are looking for a piece of information, a search engine is the place to start.

One of the most powerful "web site" search engines is at the Alta-Vista web site. Send your browser to this web address:

## http://www.altavista.digital.com

Type in a series of words that describes what you are looking for, click the Submit button, and AltaVista displays a list of web sites containing those words. For example, suppose you wanted to find a site that had pictures of the dogs from the movie *101 Dalmations*. Type in the words "disney" and "dalmations," then click Submit (or hit the Enter key).

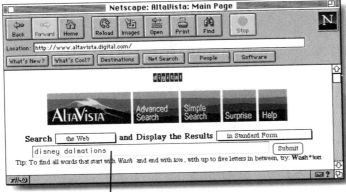

*Type in this box, then click the Submit button on the right.*

As you see below, AltaVista found about 5,000 web pages matching the words "disney" and "dalmations." AltaVista displays its results ten links at a time. To check out one of the first ten matching web pages, just click on the underlined link. To view the next ten links, click on the word "next" at the very bottom of the Alta-Vista page.

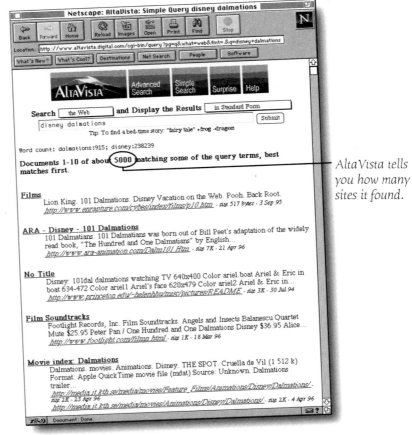

*AltaVista tells you how many sites it found.*

*We can see the first five of the first ten links this search engine found. Click on an underlined heading to jump to that site.*

While it is certainly nice that AltaVista found so many web pages containing the words "disney" and "dalmations," visiting 5,000 web pages will take the rest of your life and be very boring. Fortunately, most search engines offer a way of limiting your search. You provide more specific information to cut down your search results to a more reasonable number of pages.

For example, if you put quotation marks around "disney dalmations," AltaVista will only show you pages that have the word "disney" immediately followed by the word "dalmations." The quotes group these two words together. Without the quotes, AltaVista searches for sites that have the word "disney" somewhere on the page OR the word "dalmations" on the page.

While the quote mark technique works with most search engines, there are other ways to limit your searches. Check out AltaVista's "Advanced Search" button at the top of the page. It teaches you how to combine individual search terms using words like AND, OR, NOT, and NEAR. Many of the Internet's search engines offer similar helpful hints. Once you settle on a favorite search engine, take some time to click those Help buttons and learn how to limit your search. It will save you a great deal of time and frustration.

## Addresses for other search engines

Not all search engines will give you the same results. Most of them have their own database of information they search through, and some are very particular about what they include. For instance, when I looked for "Spam" on Yahoo, another search engine, I was informed there was no Spam on the Internet. When I used Alta-Vista (which searches differently from Yahoo), I found over 63,000 mentions of Spam. Whenever you search for something, try several different engines.

In Netscape, when you click on the "Search" button, you will get a page with links to all the major search engines. Click on any one; try them all out. If you want to go directly to the home page of a particular search engine, enter one of the URLs below.

| | |
|---|---|
| **AltaVista** | http://www.altavista.digital.com |
| **Yahoo** | http://www.yahoo.com |
| **Lycos** | http://lycos.com |
| **WebCrawler** | http://webcrawler.com |
| **InfoSeek** | http://www.infoseek.com |
| **(general)** | http://www.search.com<br>*(this site gives a brief sentence describing<br>the strengths of each of the major search engines,<br>and you can choose to search with each one from here)* |

# Going back to a page

Most web browsers keep a list of all the sites you've visited during this web browsing session. To go back to the last page you visited, click on the browser's "Back" button. To skip ahead in the list, click on the "Forward" button (see below). When you jump to a link you've found with AltaVista, you'll find it helpful to click on the "Back" button to get back to the page where AltaVista displayed the results of the search.

*Here are the Back and Forward buttons.*

In Netscape, you can also use the Go menu to return to a page you looked at a while ago. This menu keeps track of the pages you've already been to, and you can just slide down and select one to return to it. This is much faster than clicking backwards through all the pages you've viewed.

*Notice you can also use keyboard shortcuts to return to pages. In this example, wherever you are, you can press Command 2 to go back to Uncle Drag's page.*

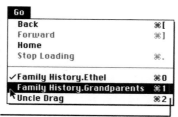

# Downloading Files

Every so often, while wandering the web you will come upon a file you just have to have on your own computer. For example, suppose you were putting together a family cookbook and you wanted to spice it up with a little artwork. You know how to search the web for cooking-related graphics, but once you find something you like, how do you get the artwork from the web site onto your own computer? By **downloading**, which means transferring the file from another computer to your computer—in this case, via the Internet.

If the artwork you are looking for is actually part of a web page (if the actual graphic appears in the web browser window), you can have your web browser save the picture as a file on your computer. If you're using Netscape, position your pointer on the desired image and *hold down the mouse button* until a pop-up menu appears (as shown below). Select "Copy this Image" from the resulting pop-up menu so you can paste the image somewhere else, or choose "Save this Image as..." and Netscape will save the file onto your hard disk.

Keep in mind, of course, that you cannot download just any old file from the Internet and use it. Although many people place their graphics on the web knowing they will be "borrowed," copyright laws still apply. It's generally okay to copy things for your personal use, but not for money-making purposes. Use common sense and be honest.

*If you press on any image in Netscape, you will see this pop-up menu. Remember when you put your own graphics on the web that anyone else will be able to grab them also. If this upsets you, don't put your graphics on the Internet.*

You might also find a **file** embedded, via a link, in a web page; that is, you don't actually see the image, but the web page tells you what it is and how to get it. For example, you might see a link that looks like this:

### Click here to download some cool cooking artwork

The word **download** is a big clue that this link is connected to a file, not to another web page.

*file: it may be a word processing document, a manual you can print from your own computer, a scanned photo, an illustration, etc. Typically, on the World Wide Web you **go** to web pages and you **download** files.*

## HTTP versus FTP

An even bigger clue that the link is connected to a file is in the address that is tied to the link. On page 41 you saw the area in your browser window that tells you the address of any link you pass your pointer over. If you want to know if a link is connected to a file or to a web page, pass the pointer over the link (don't click) and take a look at the address that appears at the bottom of the browser window (or wherever it appears in your browser). This is the **URL,** the address that tells your browser where to find a resource (like a file or web page) on the Internet.

If your URL starts with **http,** it refers to a web page.

If your URL starts with **ftp,** it refers to a file.

For example, if you click on a link with this **http** URL:

**http**://www.zumacafe.com

your browser will take you to the home page of the Internet cafe that Robin and I own, Zuma's Electronic C@fe.

*ftp: stands for file transfer protocol, which is your clue that you can download the file.*

On the other hand, here's an **ftp** URL:

**ftp**://ftp.gargoyle.com/unclefloyd/salsarecipe.txt

If this were a real URL, when you clicked on the link you would download the text of Uncle Floyd's award-winning salsa recipe.

The "ftp" stands for **file transfer protocol** (an "http" prefix stands for **hypertext transfer protocol**, which indicates the file is a page on the World Wide Web). Some browsers have a built-in ftp capability and will take care of transferring the file to your computer. Other browsers require the assistance of an **ftp helper application**, a separate program that knows how to handle file transfers. Read the documentation that came with your browser to find out which kind of browser you have. If you don't feel like reading the manual, try downloading a file and see what happens!

## Compressed files

To save download time and hard disk space, most applications are stored in a "compressed" format at the web site. Compression makes the file smaller and thus it transfers through the phone lines faster. To use the file once you've downloaded it, you'll need a helper application (page 61), such as StuffIt Expander, that knows how to uncompress your file. There are links on the Home Sweet Home Page site to several utilities for compressing and uncompressing your files.

# What's next?

In the next chapter, you'll start learning how to build your very own family and friends web site. For now, get your browser installed and make sure you can "surf" the web.

If you're using Netscape, check out the Handbook, an online tutorial written by the folks at Netscape. It will help you master the ins and outs of browsing. To read the Handbook, just click the button at the top of the Netscape screen labeled "Handbook."

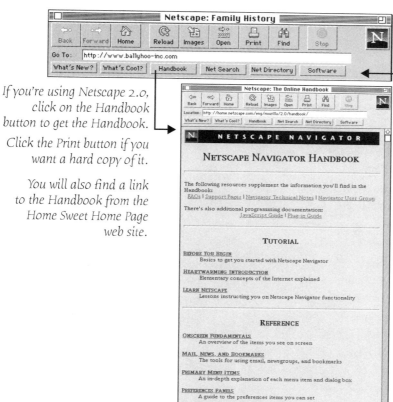

*If you're using Netscape 2.0, click on the Handbook button to get the Handbook.*

*Click the Print button if you want a hard copy of it.*

*You will also find a link to the Handbook from the Home Sweet Home Page web site.*

*If you don't see a row of buttons similar to this on your Netscape window, go to the Options menu and choose "Show Directory Buttons."*

*Also in that Options menu you see "Show Toolbar," which is what makes the upper row of buttons show up, and "Show Location," which makes the Go To/ Location box appear.*

# The Home Sweet Home Page web site

Because the information in this field is changing so incredibly fast, we have created a web site to post current information. All through this book you will find references to the Home Sweet Home Page web site for tips, tricks, how-to explanations, links, and other info that will undoubtedly be changing in the near future. What an amazing concept.

Check it out. Bookmark it. Smile.

**http://www.peachpit.com/home-sweet-home**

# Part Two

# Before & After

in which we describe
the tools you will need for creating your web site,
how to organize all the files you will be creating,
and what to do with your web site
when you are finished.

An e-mail message
is no less important
than a letter
or a phone call.

# Chapter Four
# The Tools You Need

BEFORE you can begin to create your web site, there are a couple of items you need to get: software with which to create the pages, software for making or editing graphics, and perhaps some "helper applications." Unfortunately, you cannot set up a web site with this book alone. Would that life were so easy. But this chapter does tell you what you need and where to get it, plus some tips on how to organize all the files you will be creating.

# Web authoring software

Until recently, to create a web page a designer or programmer had to learn the **hypertext markup language**, or **HTML**. This is a programming code that tells a web browser how to display the text or graphics on the screen. You can check the Appendix, "A Quick Peek at HTML," for an example of the code, but for the occasional user it is a bit overwhelming. Fortunately, a new kind of software has been developed recently: **web authoring software**. Using one of these new applications, you can create entire web sites without having to write one word of code.

So the first and foremost important tool you must acquire is a web authoring software package. My personal favorite is Adobe PageMill or SiteMill, but there are several packages available and more are being created almost daily, it seems. Rather than list them here and make this book outdated by the time it is in print, on the Home Sweet Home Page web site we have a list of the software packages available, with links to the pages where you can download them. Prices vary from free, to under $100, to expensive. They are quite easy to use.

Throughout this book we don't give very many specific how-to directions related to software that will undoubtedly change—that's what our web site is for. For each software package we provide a link to on our web site, we also provide some tips and tricks and how-to information for you. This way we can keep them up-to-date.

(And if you really want to create your web site using HTML, we have links on the web site to pages with information on writing HTML.)

So first of all, go get your web authoring software!

# Graphic programs

If you want to have graphics on your page, you must have some sort of software program in which to create them. You can draw or paint your own graphics on your computer; you can create images on paper (or on anything else—rocks, screen, metal, wood, body parts) and **scan** them; you can snatch single images from video clips; you can take photographs on any camera and scan them; you can take photographs with a digital camera and load them right into your computer; you can use clip art; you can borrow graphics from the web (as explained on page 50).

You probably already own something you could use to create and manipulate graphics. One of the most popular (and greatest) programs is Adobe Photoshop, but it's rather expensive to buy just for web graphics if you don't already own it. Adobe has a much less pricey package called PhotoDeluxe that does just about everything Photoshop does, and it is designed for beginners to use; it's great and costs less than $100. You can also use any draw or paint program, such as SuperPaint, CorelDraw, Microsoft Works, ClarisWorks, Adobe Illustrator, or Macromedia FreeHand. I have a favorite technique for using PageMaker to make many of my graphics (details are on the Home Sweet Home Page web site).

The trick, however, is to get your graphics in the right **image file format** and as small a file size as possible. Small is important because the larger the graphic, the longer it takes to display on the screen. **Graphics larger than 30K are considered large. Small icons should be no more than 2 to 5K.**

**scan:** *to get an image from the world into your computer, it must be turned into digital information so the computer can understand and display it.*

*A* **scanner** *is a piece of equipment that does this for you.*

*If you don't have a scanner, there is bound to be someone in your town who can do it for you, usually for a price.*

**file format:** *the internal structure of a graphic, how it is made. Each format has advantages and disadvantages.*

# Graphic file formats

**image file format:**
*the internal structure of a graphic, how it is made. Each format has advantages and disadvantages.*

The trick is to get your graphics in the right **image file format**. The most common file formats on the web are GIF and JPEG, both of which use "compression schemes" to make the file size small.

| | |
|---|---|
| **GIF** | Graphical Interchange Format |
| **JPEG, JPG** | Joint Photographic Experts Group |

We could go on at length about the technical advantages and disadvantages of each format, but what you probably want to know is which one to use, yes? These are the general guidelines:

Many designers use **GIFS** for drawn **graphics** such as illustrations, scanned pictures (not photos), images of text, and other graphics that can get away with a small color palette of only 256 colors. Also, there is wide support for GIFS—nearly all graphical applications accept them.

Many designers use the **JPEG** format for **photographs** because JPEGS can display "true color" (24-bit, if that means anything to you, or 16.7 million colors). It also makes a smaller file size. But keep in mind that fewer graphical applications support JPEG. (You *can* use GIFS for everything.)

*Most graphic software offers a choice of formats in which to save an image:*

**To make your graphic into a GIF or JPEG,** you need a program in which you can open the graphic and save it as one of those file formats. The easiest thing to do is open the graphic in Adobe Photoshop v3.0.5 or higher and use the Export feature to export the graphic as a GIF. Photoshop takes care of all the subtle details. A much less expensive software package that can do the same thing is Adobe PhotoDeluxe. Also check the available file formats of your current software of choice. Or go to the Home Sweet Home Page web site and download a utility called "GIF Converter" that will convert most digital graphic images into GIFS. Or ask a friend or relative to turn your graphics into GIFS or JPEGS for you.

⌂ http://www.peachpit.com/home-sweet-home

# Helpers

There are a variety of small software utilities that **help** you create and view web pages. The utilities you need today are different from what you needed last month, and the ones you may need next month have not been invented yet. Because these things change so frequently depending on the current state of the Internet, guess where you can find them—right, on the Home Sweet Home Page web site. We're not even going to name them here. But you can pop over to the web site and find links that take you to where you can download the most popular applications, plug-ins, and other utilities you'll need.

## Helper apps

Helper applications, called "helper apps," are small programs that help the web browser take advantage of the various multimedia facets of the web. Without helper apps, you may not be able to view certain movie files or animations, hear certain sounds, listen to Real Audio, or view formatted text files. Typically you must have the helper apps installed on your computer, get the file you want to hear or view, then use the helper app to hear or view the file. More and more helper apps, though, are turning into plug-ins (below).

Sparkle        SoundMachine

## Plug-ins

A plug-in extends the functionality of your web browser. It allows you to view animation or hear sounds or watch movies without having to use a helper app.

Shockwave68K

## Page production utilities

There are also links on our web site that take you to sites where you can download utilities you may find useful in the creation process, such as the GIF converter we talked about on the preceding page.

GIFConverter     SoundApp

# For right now:

To get started, all you really need is your web authoring software. If you want to add graphics to your page, you must acquire them, create them, or have someone create them for you, and make sure they are in the GIF or JPEG format.

You can get all the other things we mentioned along the way, as you find you need them. Don't let the collection of available tools daunt you—you can make your entire web site with nothing more than the web authoring software, some graphics perhaps, and your own witty text. If you have computer nerds in your family, call upon them. "Hey Emilie, could you make a video clip of this from my camcorder and write the code so we can attach it to the web site?"

http://www.peachpit.com/home-sweet-home

# Chapter Five

# Four Things to Remember

BEFORE you start creating the pages that will make your web site, there are four things you should keep in mind as you work. This chapter discusses:

⌂ Naming your web pages properly.

⌂ Titling your web pages properly.

⌂ Organizing and storing your files.

⌂ Eliminating superfluous stuff (extra graphics, text, etc.) from your web site folder.

Let's take a look at each guideline in detail.

⌂ http://www.peachpit.com/home-sweet-home

# Naming your web pages

Your software will probably allow you to name files just about anything, but you can get into trouble unless you follow the conventions listed below. Also ask your service provider if they have any special system for naming files (see pages 70–72).

⌂ Use all lowercase letters.

⌂ Use letters only, not numbers or punctuation marks.

⌂ Don't put any spaces between words, nor any capital letters.

⌂ If you need to, you can use a hyphen or the underline character (like this: _   press Shift Hyphen).

⌂ On a Macintosh, each of your web pages must have the extension **.html** after its name. For instance: **history.html**

On a PC, the extension must be **.htm**

⌂ Even if your computer lets you use a long file name, stick to a maximum of eight characters plus the extension.

**Wrong:  Our Family History!.html**

**Right:   history.html**

*extension: the letters at the end of a file name. They provide a clue as to what sort of file it is.*

## Naming graphic files

As you create your graphics, add an extension to remind you what file format it is, as in **mom.tiff** ("tiff" or "tif" is the extension). When you turn it into a GIF or a JPEG, add the appropriate extension: **mom.gif**. Before you place that graphic on a web page, make sure the file name follows all of the above conventions.

# Titling each page

Each **web page** is considered a **file**. Specifically, it is considered an HTML **file**. And that file name must use the conventions described on the preceding page. But each web page also has a **title**, a name that tells you more specifically what that page is about. For instance, the web page file *name* might be **history.html**, but the *title* is **Our Family History** (see below). You must give each page both an *HTML name* and a *title*.

Your web authoring software will ask you to **name** the file when you save it onto your hard disk. That is where you give it the HTML file name.

*When you save the page, you are **naming** it. The file must have an **htm** or **html** extension.*

There will also be a place for you to **title** the page, and that is where you can give it a more fully developed description of the page.

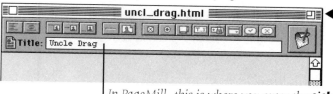

←While you are working on the file, this bar will show the file **name**. However, when you view this file in your browser, the **title** of the page will be displayed here. Try it and see.

*In PageMill, this is where you enter the **title** (press Return or Enter after you type it). In other applications you might enter the title through a "Document" dialog box or other dialog box with a similar name—look in your menus.*

# Organizing your files!

I know you haven't made any files yet, but you will save yourself so many headaches if you plan your organization right now. As you know, your pages are all linked together. When you make a link, your software writes the code that tells the browser where to find that page. The code includes the location of the other page—the name of the folder or directory it is in, the title of the page, etc.

***If you make links and then rename pages OR move them into new folders/directories, the browser will not be able to find them!***

This is very important! It means from the very beginning you must be conscious of what you are naming files and where you are storing them. You must name your folders (on a Mac) or directories (on a PC) with names you will want to keep, and you need to be consistent about where you put your files. Don't link anything to a file or graphic that is not already in its proper folder! And don't forget—your folders must also follow the naming conventions described on page 64.

When you place a graphic on your page, your web authoring software writes the code to tell the browser where that graphic is stored. If you later move the graphic from its current location into another folder, the browser cannot follow the link and the graphic won't appear on the page. In fact, your own software won't be able to find it next time you open that page on your own computer. Don't move around those graphics or pages unless you plan to go back to every page and correct the links.

 **Important note**: *Ask your "webmaster" (the person in charge of making sure your files appear on the Internet) if they have any special system for naming and organizing files and folders! Read pages 70– 72, then remember this note!*

So create a folder into which you will save the pages you are about to create (those pages are also called "HTML files"). Give the folder a logical name you will want to keep. If you plan to have a lot of graphics, make another folder inside the first folder and give it a logical name, also. It is best to create and keep these in your root directory, or right on your hard disk, not in any other folders.

*This shows the folder for a web site and some of the files within it. You can have more folders. For instance, you might want a separate folder for each section of your web site; that is, a reunion folder, a family history folder, etc. Just be sure to set them up BEFORE you start, and don't move things around or rename them after that.*

If you discover along the way that you really must move something from one folder to another, or that you have to rename a folder or a file or retitle a page, **you must go back to every affected page and relink the links**. In some instances you may have to replace the original graphic with the renamed one.

Some web authoring software packages include features that help you discover links that are not working, broken links or other problems, and provide easier ways to fix them. Read the manual!

# Eliminating superfluous stuff

Don't keep anything in your web site folder that isn't necessary for the site. For instance, you might have **word processing documents** you created in preparation for making your web pages—these do not need to be in the folder! When you typed, pasted, or dragged that text onto the web page, the text was automatically incorporated into the HTML file.

Don't keep any **graphics** in the web site folder that are not placed on a page. For instance, maybe you have a photograph you scanned as a TIFF and you did some cute stuff to it in PhotoDeluxe. Then you saved a copy as a GIF. So now you have two copies of it, one in TIFF format and one in GIF. The GIF file is the one you put on your web page, so the GIF file is the one that should be kept in the web site folder. The TIFF should be stored safely somewhere else.

If you placed a graphic on a page, then eliminated it from the page for some reason, also remove that graphic from the web site folder.

If you copied a bunch of boxes and bullets from your clip art collection but only used a couple of them, don't leave all the unused ones in the folder—keep just the images you actually used.

So when you have finished creating the web site and are ready to post it on a server (next chapter), you should have:

⌂ One folder for your web site, and in this folder you may have several other folders. These folders contain:

⌂ Only the HTML files, one for each web page.

⌂ One graphic file for each graphic on a web page.

⌂ If you use the same graphic more than once anywhere on the site, keep only **one** copy of it in the web site folder.

# Chapter Six
# When You Are Finished

AFTER you have read this book and created a wonderful web site for your family and friends, you need to "post" it somewhere. If you leave it on your hard disk, no one will ever find it. You might not be quite ready to post your pages yet, but it helps to understand where you are heading and what to expect.

# Web servers

HTML, as you may recall, stands for hypertext markup language. It is the code, written in any word processor or text editor, that tells a browser what to display on a screen. Every web page starts life as an HTML file. If you're interested, take a look at the Appendix, "A Quick Peek at HTML" for an example of what the code looks like. Most web authoring software programs write the code for you, but the result is the same—**each web page is actually an HTML file. Each HTML file is actually a web page.**

So a completed web site consists of a series of HTML files, one for each page, along with any GIF or JPEG files referenced by the HTML files. Once you have your files and images created, you are ready to bring your web site to life.

*To do this, your site must be "posted," which means you must take or send your collection of pages and images to a* **web server.** *No one can find them if they just sit on your hard disk unless you turn your own computer into a server, which I doubt you will want to do.*

A web server is a computer that contains and manages web pages. It's hooked up to the Internet 24-hours-a-day and runs special software that knows how to communicate with web browsers. The server makes the web pages available to anyone who might be looking for them over the Internet. Your pages must be "posted" to the web server so it can do that. Someone called a **webmaster** is in charge of running the server. The webmaster will take your files and do what is necessary to post them for you (don't worry—you don't have to do it yourself).

# Finding a server

Finding a full-time web server on which to post your pages is pretty easy. Both CompuServe and America Online will post your web pages if you are a member. The vast majority of Internet service providers (ISP, pages 28–29) can also store (post) your web site on a server. No matter how you are connected to the Internet, first check with your provider to see if they can post your pages on their server. If not, ask around town. Ask the local web designers where they store their clients' pages, or ask at the local Internet cafe. If your town is so small that you can't find anyone who knows anything, check the nearest larger town. Your web pages can be stored anywhere in the world! You could store them with Aunt Jean who is an ISP in Sweden. You could store them at Zuma's Electronic C@fe in Santa Fe. Also check the Home Sweet Home Page web site for a list of national providers who will store web pages. This is very rarely a free service, but the price varies quite widely. Ask around.

*Directions on how to post your pages to America Online or CompuServe can be found on each service.*

# Your very own web address

Once you have posted your pages with a web server, they will give you your very own web address. Often they can tell you what your address will be before you even finish and post your site. It may look something like:

**http://www.zumacafe.com/gargoyle-family/**

Remember the explanation of the address on pages 42–43? The "http://www" part indicates the file is a page on the World Wide Web. The "zumacafe.com" part is the domain name (pages 33–34). The "gargoyle-family/" refers to your web site on their server. Send your web address to your grandkids. Won't they be surprised.

http://www.peachpit.com/home-sweet-home

# What to post

Your service provider will set up a directory/folder on their server in which to place all your web-related files. Your job is to get all of the files that make up your web site ready to post. This will be easy if you keep everything organized from the very beginning of the creation process (golly gee, I hope you do). And I hope you remember to ask your ISP if they have any special system for naming and organizing files and folders!

⌂ Name your files properly. Don't change any names— not of graphics, pages, or folders.

⌂ Title your files properly.

⌂ Don't move items (graphics or pages) from one folder to another once you have used them on a web page or linked them to or from anywhere. (If you find you must move them, you then have to go back and re-link any files connected to that page or image before you post the site.)

⌂ Don't keep any superfluous stuff (extra graphics, text, etc.) in your web site folder.

# One more thing to do: test

Test your pages. Test your links. Make sure your graphics show up as you expect. To do this, open your Home Page with your web browser, right there on your hard disk. In most programs, you can open your Home Page by dragging its icon onto the icon of your web browser.

Go through your entire web site, clicking on every link, looking at every graphic. It may look different from what you expected (different browsers display pages differently). Don't post anything unless you have tested every link and fixed all broken ones!

# Part Three

# Get Ready
# Get Set

in which you create a map
of your web site,
decide what goes on your Home Page,
choose which pages will link
to other pages,
gather up your text and graphics,
and think about the design of your site.

Who knows
where we're goin',
but we'll
get there.

# Chapter Seven

# Make a Map

Before you begin to create your web site, it helps to make a "map" of the pages. This helps you clarify the information that will be on each of the pages, organize your ideas, establish where the **links** will be, and generally gives you a game plan so you know where you are going before you begin. You can always add or delete information, pages, and links as you go along.

**link:** *the text or graphic you click on that connects you to another page. When you click on a link, the page you are looking at disappears and you "jump" to the linked page.*

# Making a map

Remember, the World Wide Web is made of millions of individual "pages." What you are going to create are a few more pages to add to this worldwide collection. Collectively, your pages are called a "web site." I hope by now you have spent some time on the World Wide Web and have seen several web sites so you have an idea of what you are about to do!

There are several ways to make a map, depending on how you like to work. Some people are visual and prefer to make little pictures, others like to work with text. Take a look at these two methods— one of them will feel more comfortable. Or you can always use a combination—draw the pictures, then use the outline to provide more explanation of what is on each page and where it will connect.

## Your Home Page

The first page is your **Home Page**. On your Home Page you will write an introductory blurb, perhaps add a photo or two, and make links to all the other main pages in your site. On page 77, each of the rectangles in the middle column actually represents a link you will display on the Home Page. That is, there will be links to Family History, Calendar of Events, Family News, etc.

Some of the subsidiary pages will probably not be connected by a direct link from the Home Page. That is, you won't have a link to Maude's Recipes from the Home Page, but you *will* have one from the Home Page to Family Recipes. Every page in the entire web site, though, should have a link to take you *back* to your Home Page.

## A visual map

One method of creating a map is to draw little rectangles representing the pages, then draw lines linking the pages to each other. This works well for people who like to see a picture of how things connect. If you have lots of information, make sure you use a big piece of paper.

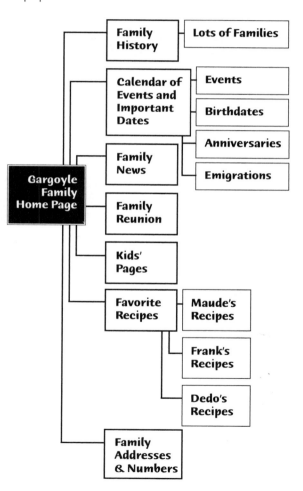

*As you work, you will probably find yourself making more and more pages—you will discover more and more information that you want to post. For instance, you might think your family reunion information will need only one page. Then as you put it together you realize you want a detailed map and directions, local hotel accommodation information, itinerary of events, a response form so members of the family can r.s.v.p., a page of the props they each need to bring for the games you are planning, requirements for the skits you expect each family to perform, a food and drink list, etc. Oh my.*

# An outline map

Another method of creating a map is to write an outline. Each major heading represents a page; each subheading represents one of the pages that links to the major head. This format allows you to use a lot more words to fully describe and develop the information that will be on the pages.

*You might decide that a combination of the two maps works best— little boxes to give you a visual picture, an outline to fill in the details.*

## Gargoyle Family Web Site

**Family History**
- Lots of families: create a separate page for each branch of the family, with a link to each one. Each page will contain not only the information of who married whom and who begat whom, but also interesting family history.

**Calendar of Events and Important Dates**
- Emigration dates: who emigrated from where, when
- Birthdates: arrange by month
- Anniversaries: arrange by month

**Family News:** this is current news of all family members, such as who is having babies, graduating, sick and needs your comfort or phone calls, off on an exciting adventure, getting married, divorcing, etc. This information is sent to or gathered by _____ and posted several times a week.

**Family Reunion:** when, where, what time, what to bring, who's coming, who needs a ride, r.s.v.p., etc.

**Kids' Pages:** this page will have links to all the pages that develop here. We should at least have pages for "Kids," "Grandkids," and "Great-Grandkids." These are playful pages, with movies, sounds, drawings, photos, stories.

**Favorite Recipes**
- Maude's recipes
- Frank's recipes
- Dedo's recipes

**Family Addresses and Numbers**
- A database of everyone's addresses, phone and fax numbers, e-mail addresses with links to their e-mail.

⌂ http://www.peachpit.com/home-sweet-home

## This is what it might look like

If you created a web site using the maps on the preceding two pages, this is what your Home Page might look like. Notice how the Home Page links to all the other pages described in the outline.

*Each of these links takes you to the first page of that section. It's kind of like going to the first page of another chapter in the same book.*

# Moving on

Okay, so now you have your map, or at least you have an idea of what you are doing and where you are going. You don't have to work in any sort of order, as long as you keep track of what has been created and what has yet to be done, and where your links are. I usually start every project by doing the easiest part first. The Home Page should be easy, then take a look at what you have on hand and decide what is the least obnoxious task. Find ways to delegate parts of the project. As you read through the rest of the information about what you should prepare, get ready to call on your family and friends. They can be gathering material for you while you map out the strategy and start creating the pages. Oh, you are going to have so much fun.

# Chapter Eight

# Prepare Your Stuff

Now, you don't *have* to get all of your text and graphics ready before you start, but it sure makes the project easier to accomplish, easier to manage, and easier to see what has been done and what needs to be done. This chapter helps you get started on that, but keep in mind that creating a web site is an organic, living, growing process. I guarantee you will think of more and more things to add to your project as you go along, and your family web site will probably be three times what you expected it to be. Ha!

# Write your text

In all **web authoring software**, you can type directly onto the page. Often, however, you might want to write a lot of the text in a word processor or "text editor" (a limited sort of word processor) so you can put together a lot of information quickly. Writing and saving your text files also ensures that you will have another copy of the text should anything catastrophic happen to your pages. If the only copy of your text is on your web site and those files are lost or damaged, you will have to start all over.

As you type the text into a word processor, **do not format anything!** That is, don't bother to change the size, the font, the style (bold, italic, etc.). Don't set any tabs or extra spaces. Don't bother to center or align to the right. Don't bother drawing any rules (lines). If someone else in your family is writing text for inclusion in the web site, be sure to tell them these restrictions!

**Don't use any special characters**, such as true apostrophes and quote marks (' or " "). Maybe you haven't even noticed if your quote marks are true or not. Well, if they are curly (as shown in the above sentence), they are true. If they are straight up and down (like this: ' or "), they are simply the dorky typewriter marks. *The Internet can only understand the dorky typewriter marks.* If the default in your word processor has been set to insert true quotes automatically, change the default so it just types the plain ol' typewriter apostrophes and quote marks (' and "). Otherwise you will confuse the authoring software. (Of course, this is guaranteed to change in the near future.)

If you know what **ASCII text** is, that's what you should use. If your software lets you save your file as "ASCII" or "Text Only," do that, then open the ASCII file to see if anything weird happened. If things changed or if you see strange characters, fix them in the ASCII file. *Any text problems you see in the ASCII file will also appear on the web page!* Fix them before you post your pages to the Internet.

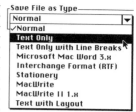

*Some applications, such as Microsoft Word, above, let you save your file as "Text Only," which is the same as "ASCII." This simply means that it strips out any offensive characters the Internet can't read or display.*

The first paragraph below is an example of formatted text, with different fonts, sizes, some bold and italic, small caps, real quotation marks, etc. Compare it with the ASCII text below it:

**GARGOYLES** were originally built into the sides of buildings in medieval times as devices to control water runoff. The word "gargoyle" comes from the French word *gargoullier,* which means to gargle, because the fixtures gargled with water. They were often made ugly, supposedly to scare away evil spirits.

Notice how plain this ASCII text appears:

```
Gargoyles were originally built into
the sides of buildings in medieval
times as devices to control water
runoff. The word "gargoyle" comes from
the French word "gargoullier," which
means to gargle, because the fixtures
gargled with water. They were often
made ugly, supposedly to scare away
evil spirits.
```

# Create your graphics

It's a good idea to get as many of your graphics together before you start. You can always add more as you go along, of course, but creating as many of the graphics as possible ahead of time helps make the project come together more smoothly.

*image file format: the internal structure of a graphic, how it is made. Each format has advantages and disadvantages. Both of the formats mentioned here can be used on any kind of computer.*

On page 60 you learned about the two popular **image file formats** that the most common web **browsers** can display:

| | |
|---|---|
| **GIF** | Graphical Interchange Format |
| **JPEG, JPG** | Joint Photographic Experts Group |

You can create or get images from many places, such as paint or drawing programs, scanners, video capture, digital cameras, clip art, etc. If there is no one in your family who knows how to make digital art, you can find someone you can pay or trade to do it. Check the yellow pages of your phone book for ad agencies, graphic designers, or typesetting service bureaus. Or ask your Internet service provider if they can give you the names of people who can create web graphics for you. Ask at your local Internet cafe. Before you hire someone, though, read page 90 and try drawing some things yourself. You'll be surprised at what you can do.

However you do it, get your graphics ready. They should be in GIF or JPEG format (page 60) and properly named (page 64). Of course, you can always create more graphics as you develop your site!

# Chapter Nine

# Design the Pages

This chapter is a very brief introduction to some basic design ideas and a few ways to make your pages sparkle. The point of the whole chapter is that you can't be a wimp. Go for it. Do it. Be bold. Don't be boring. Put some thought into how your pages look. Have fun. Do something unexpected. You are publishing this for the world! Make a statement!

# Get some new fonts

fonts: *typefaces. There are thousands of different typefaces. Many are available free on online services such as America Online or CompuServe. Ask your local user group where you can buy more fonts; ask your friends;check the Home Sweet Home Page web site.*

Really. It is amazing what the investment in a couple of **fonts** (typefaces) can do for your page. Now, you can't use your great fonts as text when putting together your pages! Every person browsing at their own computer decides what typeface they want their browser to display text with on the web pages. If you buy some weird font, you can bet your booty very few people have that typeface as their chosen web font. No one will ever see it if you type with it in your web authoring software. (As with everything else, this also is changing. Someday soon you will be able to specify the fonts on the page.)

**But**, you *can* use that font in graphics. You can make your headlines into graphics, then drop those graphics onto the pages.

*Check the Home Sweet Home Page web site for information on how to obtain these two fonts (ha! if you want them!).*

## This is the typeface Gargoyle (I made it).

## And this is MudBug, by John Tollett.

Take a look at the examples on the next page. The first headline is in the rather generic font called Times, or Times Roman, which is what most people browse in. You can set that on your page easily and instantly, but see what a different impression you get by using a different typeface, as in the other examples. Pretend this piece of type is for the Home Page, the very first page a person sees. Which best represents the family?

http://www.peachpit.com/home-sweet-home

The
# Gargoyle Family
Home Page

The
## Gargoyle Family
Home Page

*Which of the other examples do you think gives the best impression of the Gargoyle family? Ah, now don't jump to stereotypes! You have never actually met this family. Perhaps the froufrou font (third one down, typeface is called ITC Scriptease) is the most representative. You never know. Or the last one – maybe they are all bankers and lawyers.*

*Or perhaps the attraction of one typeface over another is that one is in direct contradiction to what you expect.*

*Whether you choose lovely fonts or ugly fonts, just follow this guideline:*

**Don't be boring.**

*Even if you don't have a clue about how to design with type, just choose a bold, provocative, or exciting face and do it.*

## Which would you choose?

The World Wide Web is a very graphic medium, and it is the first time that many of us can afford to produce things in color! The common masses (that's us) are finally attracted to the Internet because it is finally visually pleasing (it used to be plain ol' computer text). So, with that in mind, which of the headlines below would you find yourself more interested in, more attracted to, more likely to read?

It takes very little trouble to make some graphic text. Learn to do it—you'll be rewarded and empowered!

*The graphic for the page on the right was created simply and easily in ClarisWorks. It's just strong fonts on a dark box. You can do that.*

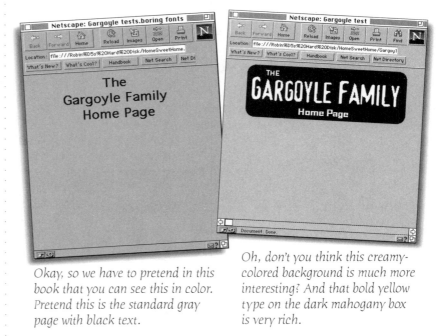

*Okay, so we have to pretend in this book that you can see this in color. Pretend this is the standard gray page with black text.*

*Oh, don't you think this creamy-colored background is much more interesting? And that bold yellow type on the dark mahogany box is very rich.*

# Don't be afraid to use color!

Our eyes are attracted to color, and color on the web doesn't cost any more than black-and-white. You've probably noticed, if you've been on the web at all, that you tend to be more attracted to the pages that catch your eye with color. Now, you can just add color to your text on the page, but you'll create a greater impact if you sneak it in in a couple of other ways.

## Headlines as colorful graphics

Fun, provocative, and colorful headlines make an amazing difference to your family web site. All the other text and information can be plain ol' black Times Roman, but those interesting headlines add quite a spark to the page. Almost everyone has a drawing program of some sort on their computer, such as ClarisWorks, CorelDraw, Microsoft Works, SuperPaint, etc. It is beyond the scope of this book to teach you how to use those programs, but if you have even the most rudimentary of skills you can make colorful type on a black or colored background box.

## Make some drawings!

Even the most primitive graphics add interest to your page. If you have artistic talent, go for it. But even crude, silly drawings can make your pages more appealing. Don't be shy. If your drawings are dorky, so what!! Make them colorful! Make them fun! Revel in their dorkiness! As John Grimes, the famous cartoonist, said, "I was amazed to discover that I can draw badly very well."

Use your paint or draw program and make some fun, silly, colorful drawings to illustrate items on your pages.

*Now really, don't these dumb little drawings have a lot of character? Go ahead and make your own!*

http://www.peachpit.com/home-sweet-home

## Use clip art

Of course, you can use **clip art**, which comes in all sorts of styles. There are many sources of clip art. To make it easier to create your web page, buy a clip art package that has been created especially for the World Wide Web (check the Home Sweet Home Page web site for suggestions). Web graphics have been optimized and changed to the appropriate format that is necessary for use on a web page—you don't have to fuss with anything. Regular clip art is usually in an "eps" format, which you cannot use on the Web; you must first convert it to a GIF or JPEG (see page 60).

It's generally a good idea to use one style of art on your pages so they present a cohesive whole. That is, if you like the woodcut style, use woodcut clip art throughout your site. If you prefer abstract art, use abstract art throughout your site. But don't let that guideline stop you—it's more important that you have fun, enjoy what you're doing, and use whatever graphics you have!

**clip art**: *little drawings, such as those shown below, that a professional artist has created. You can buy clip art on a disk and use it any way and anywhere you like.*

*Be sure to read the section on graphics to make sure the ones you want to use can be seen on the web (see page 60).*

*These are examples of some of the rules, boxes, and bullets you might find in web clip art.*

## Use graphic lines or boxes

Often the information on a web page is separated by lines (called "rules" in graphic jargon), and items may have little "bullets" or boxes in front of them. Using rules, bullets, boxes, or arrows in color is another way to add colorful interest to your page. You can create them yourself in your paint program, or you can use clip art. Most web authoring software comes with a variety of pieces you can use, or, as I mentioned before, check the Home Sweet Home Page web site for suggestions on where to get current clip art collections.

You can also use bullets (or any tiny graphic you create or find) to make rules across the page—just insert a bunch of them in a row. Or if you have a centered alignment on your page, try centering just three bullets as a divider. Or try a bullet on either side of a graphic. As you browse the Web, look for ways others have used bullets, boxes, rules, and arrows effectively. Also look for those pages where bullets and boxes clutter up the page or make it look junky! We learn as much from our awareness of the bad stuff as we do from our awareness of the good.

http://www.peachpit.com/home-sweet-home

## Background patterns and colors

One easy way to add an instant and strong impact to your page is to color the background or add a pattern instead of just using the default gray of the web page. One easy way to destroy your page and make people gag is to use the wrong color or pattern. Follow this simple rule: **If it looks hard to read, _IT IS_**. How many pages have you seen on the web where people put small type on a busy background? The background may have a strong impact, but if people have to struggle through your text, they will leave. The plain ol' type is hard enough to read on the screen; don't do silly things to make it worse.

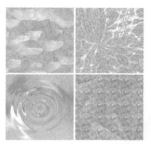

_These are a few samples of background patterns. Notice how light they are, even though some have interesting textures and colors._

Lack of contrast between the text color and the background color also make it difficult to read, such as orange type on a red background. Don't snort—I have seen this. Not only will it be difficult to read, but people will snicker disdainfully at you and your pages.

_This is an example of a really dumb background._

Using different background patterns and colors is an easy way to tie together separate parts of your site. In the Gargoyle web site, for instance, we might want to color all the Family History pages pale mint green, and all of the recipe pages a light tan. This gives the reader a subtle clue that the pages are related to each other, they are one "chapter."

However, you can only get away with using different colors on each page or in each section if there is something on every page in the site that unifies the whole thing, that tells the viewer all of these pages really belong to one bigger unit, one "book." Your unifying factor might be the style of the headlines, the format, or a consistent graphic across the top. Create some binding element that readers will recognize, then feel free to be a little more wild with some of the other elements.

# Create contrast

The principle of "contrast" is one of the most important in all design. Contrast allows us to read—setting different *values,* or darknesses, of color next to each other. If there is not a strong difference in the value of the text and the value of the page, then we cannot read the text whether it is on the screen or in a book. For instance, black type on a dark blue background is difficult to read because both black and dark blue are very dark values; white text and a gray background are both very light values, as is pale yellow text on a white background. Even black type on a very busy background can be impossible to read. Don't do it!

So we need to build contrast into the page as a basic requirement for readability. This might seem like common sense, but it's surprising how often it's neglected, especially on web sites.

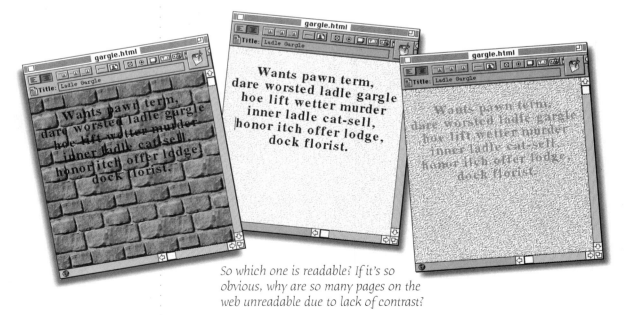

*So which one is readable? If it's so obvious, why are so many pages on the web unreadable due to lack of contrast?*

Contrast appeals to us, we look toward it. If a page has a bland, flat look, we won't stay very long unless we are intensely interested in the text (as in a novel—while reading a novel, we don't *want* to be distracted by visual interest on the page).

Contrast in other forms, such as contrast of spatial relationships, size, boldness of type, etc., not only makes a page more inviting, **the contrast makes it easier to find the information you seek on the page**. Contrast helps create good communication.

Below, both examples contain the same text. Which page are your eyes attracted to? Which page are you more inclined to spend more time on? Before you read the captions, spend a moment trying to put into words why one page is more inviting and communicates more clearly.

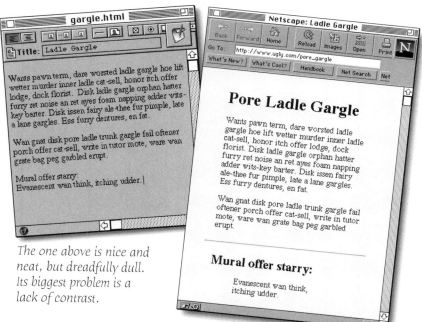

*The one above is nice and neat, but dreadfully dull. Its biggest problem is a lack of contrast.*

*There's really nothing fancy going on here—just take your common sense and put it to use.*

*On the right, there is more contrast between the type and the color of the page. A large headline has been created. A rule (line) has been added to visually separate the story and its "mural." The mural subhead is larger and bolder (adding contrast in both ways). These bold heads make it easy to skim the page and absorb the gist of it.*

*The indent also provides a contrast, giving the mural itself special yet subtle attention.*

# Let there be space

Another feature that makes great pages is **space**–empty space, resting space, defining space. But space just hanging around all over the place can also make a page appear cluttered. The trick to using space (or "white space," as designers call it) effectively is to **organize it**. If you align all your elements, your space will automatically be in the right place. Empty space scattered hither and thither tends to break up the page, forcing apart the separate elements. Learn to see the white space as another element on the page that needs to be carefully placed. Notice how good designers have used empty space on web sites, notice its organization. The more you consciously notice good design, the more it will flow back out of you.

*Compare this page with the one opposite. Point out the differences between the page with organized elements and the page without.*

*Notice how keeping items aligned (lined up) helps communicate the information at a glance. (Added contrast in the headlines also helps.) Our eyes like things to be organized–it seems to make us happy. Organizing the text and graphics automatically organizes the white space.*

*In this example there are trapped chunks of white space scattered all over the page.*

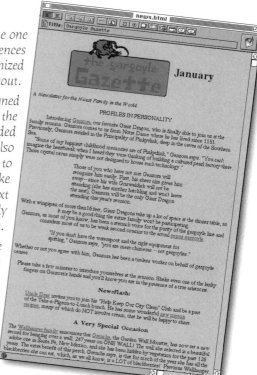

# Clean pages are good pages

No matter what is on your pages, whether they have lots of text with a variety of headlines, lots of graphics or no graphics, lists or bulleted directories, the important image to project is "clean." What makes a clean page? There can be lots of stuff on a page and yet it still appears clean and professional *if it is not cluttered.*

To prevent all the elements from becoming cluttered, **choose one alignment and stick to it**. That is, don't center some things and align others on the left, with still other elements centered and indented. Pick one alignment and use it on the entire page, perhaps with some indenting to organize and define information. You can see the difference it makes in this example. Watch for it on web pages as you surf.

*If you haven't already read it, I recommend another one of my books, The Non-Designer's Design Book (by Robin Williams). It's easy. The design principles in it apply to any printed page, whether on the web, in a book, on a flyer, or on a matchbox.*

*Notice where the white space creates a pleasing resting place, where it prevents crowding, and where it helps define the organization. Adding more space on a web page is free. Let it be there! But the empty space should also be organized.*

*The great thing is, though: if you organize the other elements, the white space will be where it is supposed to be. Trust it.*

news.html

Title: Gargoyle Gazette

the gargoyle
**Gazette**    January

*A Newsletter for the Nicest Family in the World*

**Personality Profile: Ganzora**

Introducing Ganzora, our favorite Giant Dragon, who is finally able to join us at the family reunion. Ganzora comes to us from Notre Dame where he has lived since 1151. Previously, Ganzora resided in the Principality of Pinkydink, deep in the caves of the Southern Sea.

"Some of my happiest childhood memories are of Pinkydink," Ganzora says. "You can't imagine the heartbreak when I heard they were thinking of building a cultured pearl factory there. Those crystal caves simply were not designed to house such technology."

Those of you who have not met Ganzora will recognize him easily. First, his cheer one gives him away—since his wife Gnawlakish will not be attending (she has another hatchling and won't leave the nest), Ganzora will be the only Giant Dragon attending this year's reunion.

With a wingspan of more than 16 feet, Giant Dragons take up a lot of space at the dinner table, so it may be a good thing the entire family won't be participating. Ganzora, as most of you know, has been a staunch voice for the purity of the gargoyle line and considers most of us to be weak second cousins to the actual genus gargoyle.

"If you don't have the waterspout and the right equipment for spring," Ganzora says, "you are mere chimeras — not gargoyles."

Whether or not you agree with him, Ganzora has been a tireless worker on behalf of gargoyle causes. Please take a few minutes to introduce yourselves at the reunion. Shake even one of the lanky fingers on Ganzora's hands and you'll know you are in the presence of a true aristocrat.

**Newsflash:**

Uncle Drac invites you to join his "Help Keep Our City Clean" Club and be a part of the Take-a-Pigeon-to-Lunch bunch. He has some wonderful new pigeon recipes, many of which do NOT involve cream, that he will be happy to share.

**A Very Special Occasion**

# Be smart about your links

People are going to navigate around your pages through your links, so your link system becomes part of the active design. It's critical that you make your links as clear and easy as possible. Here are some points to remember:

Map of Web Site:

Gargoyle Family
Home Page

Family History

Calendar of Events
and Important Dates

Family News

Family Reunion

Kids' Pages

Favorite Recipes

Family Addresses
& Numbers

On your Home Page, don't make a link to *every* other page in your site (unless you only have two or three other pages). Group pages together into sets and subsets. For instance, if you follow the example of the map on page 77 (recreated in the sidebar to the left), your Home Page would have links to the first pages of the Family History section, Calendar of Events, Family News, Family Reunion, Kids' Pages, Favorite Recipes, and the Family Addresses and Numbers. Each of those separate sections will have links to the other pages in their own sections.

But—the reader should be able to return to the Home Page *from wherever they happen to be.* Next time you are cruising the web, take note of how others have set it up for you to navigate through their site. Many sites have a special strip of buttons repeated on every page that link you back to the first pages of each section.

Some of your pages might be long and the reader will have to scroll up and down to find the information. For instance, you might have a database of all the numbers and addresses and e-mail links of every family member, which could be quite a long list. Rather than make the reader scroll through the entire page, up and down and up and down, have a link after each address that will take the reader back to the "Top" of the page or Home.

Also, people often put links to the other main sections in logical places on a long page so you can always jump to wherever you need to be next from wherever you happen to be at the moment.

⌂ http://www.peachpit.com/home-sweet-home

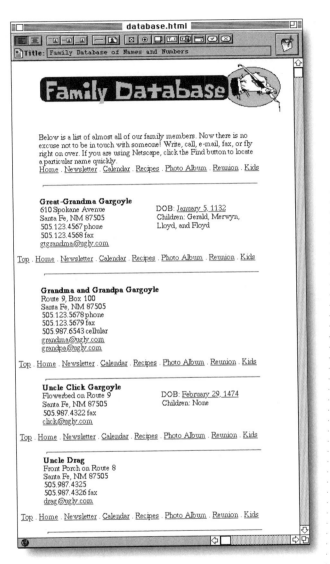

**anchor**: *a special link that takes you to somewhere else on the same page, as opposed to jumping you to another page altogether.*

*On this page example, the links to "Top" are all anchors targeted to the top of the page. In most applications you just need to make one anchored link and then copy it to all the other necessary locations.*

*Although this page is about four feet long, you can always jump back to Home from wherever you may be on the page, or to the beginning of each of the other sections. Again, once you set up the links, you can copy and paste them into other positions on this page or on any other page.*

# Don't be a wimp

The most important rule of all design (and of Life) is "Don't be a wimp." Make a statement. Be bold. Be colorful. Use your silly drawings. Use a provocative font. Use color. Make things big. Make things small. Even if you want a more sedate appearance to your pages, you can still be strong in the clean look, even in the severity of its austerity. Don't be boring.

# Part Four

# Simply Great Projects!

in which you create your Home Page
and several other pages
for your family web site,
then link them all together.

# Important:
# web authoring software!

I hope you read Chapter 4 regarding the web authoring software you need so you can make your web site. Please let me remind you that there are many programs available, more are appearing all the time, they are changing rapidly, and there is no way this book could provide up-to-date, step-by-step, how-to instructions for even one application, let alone all of them. Thank goodness for the World Wide Web. Remember, you can go to the Home Sweet Home Page web site and print or download current tips and tricks and step-by-step directions for several software choices. There are even links on the page that take you to the sites where you can download the software itself. The web authoring packages all work in a similar way, so if you are the least bit familiar with your software then you won't have any trouble at all creating these projects.

# How do you do it?

As we said before, it is not possible to give step-by-step directions for every web authoring program on the market. And besides, this book would be out-of-date in a week if we did that. But trust me, these programs are simple to use, and they all follow the same principles. I must assume that since you are ready to create a web site, you are familiar with the basics of how to use your computer. You know how to use the mouse and menus, how to copy and paste, how to create and save your text files, and how to find them again, etc.

The first several projects walk you through the different parts of creating a web site, such as starting your first page, formatting your text, making a second page, linking the two pages together, using tables, creating anchors that link you to another spot on the same page, adding graphics, etc. Once you've worked your way through the first three projects, the rest will be easy since they are simply more of the same.

You really should go to the **Home Sweet Home Page web site**, though, and find the tips and tricks for your particular web authoring software before you begin. Adobe PageMill, for instance, can be a little fussy and you **must** do four things before you begin to create your site or it won't work right (create and name a folder, set your preferences to default to that folder, save the Home Page with the name *index.html*, and title the page itself with a name like "Gargoyle Home Page"; details on the web site).

**http://www.peachpit.com/home-sweet-home**

# Alright already, let's go!

Okay, okay—so you're ready to begin. You should have these items available now:

The software you need to create the pages (page 58).

A map of your family web site (pages 76–78).

The text for your Home Page (pages 82–83).

The text (or ideas, anyway) for the rest of your pages.

The graphics (photos, illustrations, clip art, etc.) you want on your pages, in the appropriate format (pages 59–60, 84).

As we create the pages, I will be telling you about other software you might want to add to your collection, such as the things you need for creating and listening to sounds so your kids can send messages to their grandparents, or so your dogs can send messages to your kids. Remember, you can always download any of the software we mention by going to the Home Sweet Home Page web site and following the links.

# Project One
# Your Home Page

Your Home Page, as you probably well know by now, is the first page of your web site. It is the page people will go to when they type in your **web address** (your **URL**). If your entire site is going to consist of one page, then this Home Page will be it—you will place your text and graphics on the page and "post" it.

But if you plan to have more than one page, then this Home Page will have links that direct people to the additional pages. It should have a heading clearly announcing your family name. This might be a good time to invent your coat of arms or develop a logo for your name. Your logo can be simply an interesting typeface on a colored background, as you saw on page 87. Don't be shy!

You might also have a brief bio of your family, and perhaps a photo or some other image or illustration that personifies your family. If you don't have a family photo that includes everyone, you might want a photo of the family dog or cat instead so no one's feelings get hurt. Or one photo of the matriarch and/or patriarch of your clan. Or a piece of clip art that might relate to your family. Or simply your interesting coat of arms or new family logo you just created. Spend some time thinking of the appropriate image. Try to go beyond the most obvious. I know you're creative!

**web address:** *the string of text people type in to get to your web site. It's the same principle as the address of your house. Your web address will start with* **http://www**. *See pages 42–43 for more info on web addresses.*

*How do you know what your web address is? See page 71.*

http://www.peachpit.com/home-sweet-home

# Home Page ideas

Below are a couple of ideas for your Home Page. Notice this page does not include a link to every single page in your site, but to the major categories. Once you click on a link and go to that page, you will find links to the individual pages within that group.

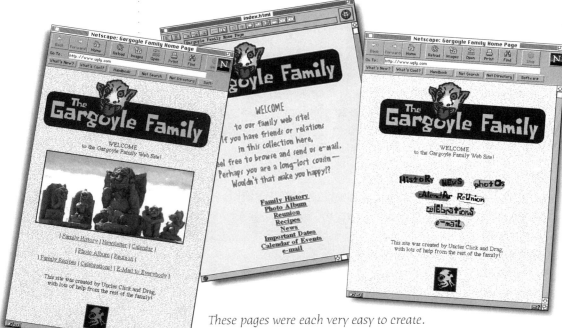

*These pages were each very easy to create. A fancy font and a piece of clip art on a dark box for the title; perhaps a photo; perhaps fancy buttons easily created with type on colored boxes. Everything is safely centered. There is nothing here you can't do!*

# Start now!

Okay, you're ready. Your graphics are assembled. Your text is written on your computer or on a piece of paper, or you know what you are going to write directly on the web page.

1. Create a new folder or directory into which you will store only the **pages** you create and the **graphics** that are on them. You do not need to keep any text files in this folder!

gargoyle.site

As you create new **web pages** with your web authoring software, this is where you should save and keep them.

After your **graphics** are in the proper format, this is where you should keep them.

**Do not** put anything unnecessary in this folder, because this is the folder you will take or send to your service provider (see pages 69–72 for details about where to send your files when you are done).

**Keep all other files** related to your web site in another folder, including your original text files, original graphics that are not in the JPEG or GIF format, graphics you didn't use on any page, practice elements, etc.

*Be sure to read page 64 regarding the proper way to name your files!*

*The folder that actually holds the web site files contains **only** web site files—nothing superfluous!*

*Keep another folder for all the **extra** files you create in the process—original graphics, all the text, etc.*

2. Open your software (double-click on its icon).

PageMill™          NaviPress          Netscape Navigator Atlas

*These are icons from some of the web authoring software packages.*

3. From the File menu, choose the item that makes a new page (it might be "New" or "New Page" or "New File," etc.).

4. Always **save** and **name** the page right away, before you do anything. This is not only a precautionary measure that helps prevent your computer from crashing and saves your boompah when you *do* crash, but most programs cannot write the HTML code if the file has not been saved.

**HTML:** *stands for hypertext markup language (see page 175).*

*You are using one of the software programs that lets you create web pages without having to write the darn code.*

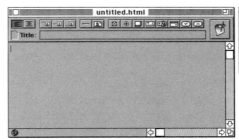  

*If the title bar in your window says "untitled," you probably haven't saved it yet.*

Check with your service provider or whoever is going to store your web site. This is critical! Usually home page files must be named either **index.html** or **default.html**, or perhaps they need the **.htm** extension instead of **.html**. Ask your webmaster (page 70) how they prefer you name your home page.

If you start creating a web site with pages that link to your home page, but then you change the name of the home page file, you are setting yourself up for lots of trouble later when the links can't find the page.

5. **Title** the page. There might be a box at the top of the page in which you can type the title, or look for a menu item called something like "Document," where you can type in a title. Give it a name you will recognize, a name that refers to what is on the page. You will probably want to title your home page something like **Gargoyle Family Home Page**.

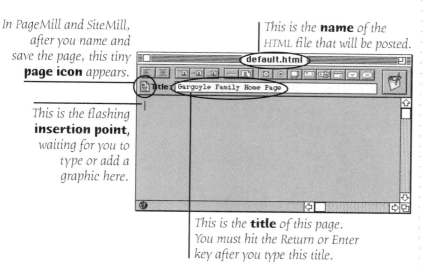

In PageMill and SiteMill, after you name and save the page, this tiny **page icon** appears.

This is the flashing **insertion point**, waiting for you to type or add a graphic here.

This is the **name** of the HTML file that will be posted.

This is the **title** of this page. You must hit the Return or Enter key after you type this title.

Now, don't let this confuse you, but the HTML **file name** is displayed right here **only while you are working on the page**.

When you or anyone else views this same page on the browser, the **title** of the page will be displayed here! That's why it's important to give the page a **title** people will understand, one that explains the document.

**6.** Now you're ready to type information on your page. So type! An **insertion point** (a short vertical line, shown on the preceding page) should be flashing on the web page, which is your clue that the document is waiting for you to type or add graphics.

You can type directly on the page, or if you have text in another document, you can open that document, copy the information, then paste that text onto the web page.

## Edit and browse modes

Most applications have two ways of working with the pages: **edit mode**, for creating and changing the page, and **browse mode** for checking your links. Make sure you are in the edit mode before you start typing.

Edit mode    Preview, or Browse mode

Edit mode    Preview, or Browse mode

*In Adobe PageMill or SiteMill, the icon on the left indicates you are in Edit mode, where you can type, add graphics, make links, etc.*

*Click on the icon to switch into the Preview/Browse mode, where you can check your links. Click again to switch back to editing.*

*Or you can toggle between Edit and Browse modes by pressing Command Spacebar on a Mac, Control Spacebar on a PC.*

*In Netscape Navigator Atlas, when you **see** the Browse button, it means you are currently in the Edit mode— click on the Browse button to go into Browse/Preview mode to check your links.*

*When you **see** the Edit button it means you are in Browse mode—if you click the Edit button, you will leave Browse mode and go into Edit mode where you can type, add graphics, make links, etc.*

# Add your graphics

First, of course, you must prepare your graphics properly, as was explained on pages 60 and 84. Put them in your graphic folder.

⌂ If they are GIFS or JPEGS, put the images in the folder in which you are keeping all the graphic files for your site.

⌂ If they are PICTS on a Mac and you are planning to drag them onto a PageMill or SiteMill page, store the PICTS in a separate, unrelated folder. When you drag one onto a page, PageMill or SiteMill will make a GIF copy of the image and put the GIF in your preferred graphics or web site folder for you.

⌂ If the graphics are in any other format besides GIF or JPEG, first turn them into the proper format or you will not be able to add them to your web site.

Then you need to find the command in your software that brings in the graphics. For instance, in Netscape Navigator Atlas, click on the Insert Image button (see right) to get the dialog box that navigates you to the file you need. Or you can choose "Image…" from the Insert menu. In PageMill or SiteMill, you can also add a graphic by clicking on a little "Insert Image" button (see right), or you can just drag a JPEG or GIF from its folder to the page and drop it where you want it. *The image will be inserted where your insertion point is flashing, so watch that insertion point!*

*This is the Insert Image button in Netscape Navigator Atlas.*

*This is the Insert Image button in PageMill and SiteMill.*

If you didn't do it in your graphics program (where you should have), you can usually resize the image right on the web page. It might be as easy as selecting an image and dragging a corner handle (hold the Shift key down so you don't drag it out of proportion), or you might have to go to a dialog box and enter the new size you want. Also, always try double-clicking on a graphic to see what options are offered.

⌂ http://www.peachpit.com/home-sweet-home

# Creating the rest of your pages

As you read through the rest of this book, you will be learning more about the various techniques and principles of creating your web pages, but the basic procedure is going to follow what you learned in this chapter:

- ⌂ Make a **new page**,
  **save it** with an appropriate name,
  and **title it**.

- ⌂ Add your **text**.

- ⌂ Add your **graphics**.

Then there is just one more step:

- ⌂ Once you have several pages,
  you need to **link** them to each other.

When you think you are finished, **test** the links! See page 72.

# Linking the pages together

Listed below are the four most common links you will be making, either from text or graphics. To make these links, you should READ THE MANUAL, as the procedures vary slightly from program to program. After you create a link, your text will be underlined and colored, and a graphic will have a border around it. (This does not necessarily mean you did it right and that the link works!)

1. Link from one page in your web site to another page in the **same site**.

   This link may be as easy to create as dragging an icon from one page onto another page (as in PageMill or SiteMill). Or it may involve navigating through a list of files in a dialog box to find the page you need to link to.

2. Link from one page in your web site to a page in **another web site**, anywhere in the world.

   This involves typing in the URL of the page you want to link to, which of course means you must know the address of that page! You might have it already written down somewhere, or you may have to go that site to get its exact address. Once you've verified the correct address by using it to get to the site, select the URL in the location box, copy it, and paste it somewhere safe until you are ready to make a link with it.

3. On a long page, you might have a special link called an **anchor** (page 99) that takes the reader from one part of that page to another part of the **same page**.

   Anchors can be a wee bit tricky, as you generally must first place the anchor, then target the text or graphic to that anchor. Read the manual!

**Test your links!**
*Always, before you post your site, check every link on every page. Go into Browse mode and click on all of them (except the ones that go to pages outside your web site). The more sophisticated software applications have features for checking your links without having to do it manually—read your manual.*

*After you have checked the links using your web authoring software,* **open the site with your browser** *(drag your home page file on top of the browser icon).* **Test all the links and check the graphics again**.

⌂ http://www.peachpit.com/home-sweet-home

4. An **e-mail** link pops up an e-mail form instead of jumping you to another page or part of a page.

This is easy. Select the text on your page that says, "E-mail me!" or "me@address.com" and in the space provided in your software for writing in links, type in:

**mailto:**

and then type in the e-mail address of the person. Click an OK button if there is one, or hit Return or Enter. For instance, if the e-mail was to me, I would enter:

**mailto:robin@zumacafe.com**

Yes, "mailto:" is one word, use a colon, and don't type a space after the colon. The e-mail address must have an @ symbol in it (pronounced "at"), or it's not an e-mail address!

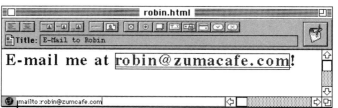

*In SiteMill, I selected the text to which I want to apply the e-mail link. I typed* **mailto:robin@zumacafe.com** *in this bottom link box and hit the Return or Enter key. The text changed color and is underlined, indicating the link has been applied.*

There are other links, such as **image map** links for creating several links on one graphic image, but they are a little trickier. Check your manual for the specific steps to creating image map links in your software application of choice, and talk to your webmaster.

# Using tables

Several of the projects in this book use tables. If you've ever used the table feature in any other program, you'll find the concept works pretty much the same here. There are "cells" into which you type, and you can have rows and columns of cells. You can show the borders in varying thicknesses, or you can turn them off altogether so your type just appears to be in columns. Tables are very handy for all sorts of projects.

Basically, in your program you just need to find the menu item called "Tables." (duh.) You will be asked how many columns and how many rows, and perhaps some other self-explanatory questions. On the web page, click in the first cell to add an insertion point, then type. The cell will expand as you type, and you can always tell the columns and rows to be wider or narrower if necessary, often by just dragging an edge of the column, or perhaps through the table menu commands. You do not have to type in every cell.

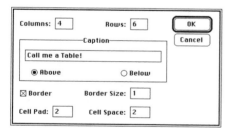

*This is an example of what the table dialog box might look like. Experiment with the numbers in the boxes, or read the manual to find out exactly what to enter for each of the options.*

You can also add graphics to cells, and you can even have a combination of type and graphics. Tables are very flexible and are a great tool for designing, especially if you have a variety of information to present, as in a family web page. Keep your eyes open as you cruise the web and notice where and how other people have used tables in their work. There are a couple of examples of tables on the following page.

## Examples of tables

These examples are screen shots from the web. Many layouts where you see things in columns are actually tables with a border setting of 0 (zero). Notice how you can use tables to avoid the all-centered look of a page.

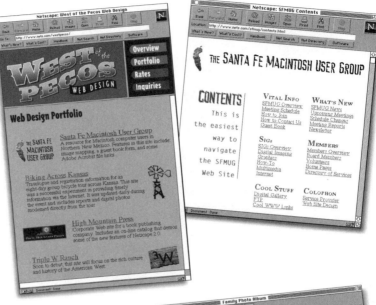

*This is an example of a table with the borders turned on. You can see this same table with the borders turned off on page 132. Tables are easy to create and very effective.*

# Project Two

# Your Family History

Some people know a great deal about their family history, and some know almost nothing. It might be surprising how much you can un-cover when you go digging around. (Check out the genealogy links on the Home Sweet Home Page web site.) You are probably going to have to do some work to gather the historical information, but this is valuable. It is worth the time and energy. When you put your page up, you might want to ask for help and input online. If you have an unusual name, relatives of yours might come out of the cyber-woodwork.

The history of your family can take several forms. A traditional family tree, of course, shows your lineage back through the ages—who married whom, who begat whom, and so on. It is very difficult at this point in the evolution of the software to design a traditional family tree on a web page. So we must become creative and inno-vative. If you really want a traditional tree, one possibility is to draw your family tree on paper, scan it, and import it as a graphic. You can then create an **image map** of links so people can click on a

**image map**: *a graphic image with invisible shapes on it that are actually buttons that link to other pages. When the pointer is over a button, it turns into the hand with the pointing finger—this is your clue that there is a link to be clicked upon. It is a good idea to also create matching text links.*

name in the tree to go to a corresponding page with more information about that person or family. If you are very clever with your drawing or painting software, you can create the tree as a graphic and put it on the page. Both of these possibilities could make lovely, interesting images, but most family trees, if they go back very far, are too large and cumbersome for a web page.

This chapter walks you through a more appropriate way to display your family tree and history, one that takes advantage of the medium, and at the same time allows you to develop each branch of the tree in a much richer and more interesting way than simply as an array of lifeless names.

If you have a large family, I suggest you start with one set of grandparents to keep the site manageable. For instance, just from my Grandma and Grandpa Williams we now have a family of 55 people, give or take a few ex-husbands and wives, new boyfriends, step-kids, etc. Thanksgiving is quite an event. So I would make a Williams site with family history for that side of the family, then make a separate site for the Weber side of the family (my mother's side, my other grandparents). But of course, we can all link our related sites together and who knows—if we follow all the links, you and I might end up being related! After all, General Colin Powell and Princess Diana are distant cousins.

# The web version of a family tree

If you're ready, follow these steps for creating the history section of your family web site. This may be one of the largest sections of your site. If your family is small, you don't need to make a bunch of separate pages—you could put them all on one page with links and anchors that pop you around that one page, as shown on pages 98–99. Let's pretend you will be making several separate pages.

⌂ In your web authoring software, create a new page just like you did for your Home Page.

⌂ In your paint or draw program, create a headline for this page, something like "Gargoyle Family History." Put that on the web page. Or if you prefer, just type it directly on the page and make it a large size, perhaps with a rule beneath.

⌂ Type a short paragraph explaining what this page (or collection of pages) is about.

*Notice the words "Grandma and Grandpa Gargoyle" are underlined. This indicates the phrase is linked to another page. Don't worry about this yet.* **You cannot link to a page until you create that page.** *We'll do that later.*

⌂ **Now create a new**, **separate page** for these grandparents. On this new page, type a headline (or add a graphic headline). Type their history, how they met, where they lived, add all the photos you can dig up, and the names of each of their children. If they are no longer alive, add the memories and reminiscences of people who knew and loved them. Or hated them. Make it interesting.

*Later, after you have created the pages for other family members, you can link them from here. Notice the links on this web page (the underlined text).* **After** *you create those pages, you can link them.*

⌂ The names of their children (one of these children, of course, is your parent) are each linked to *their* own history pages. That is, let's say Grandma and Grandpa had three children: twin boys, Click and Drag, and a lovely daughter, Ethel Frances. Well, each of these children has a link to their own history page, telling anecdotes about their lives, photos of growing up, how they met their partners, what they do for a living, and the names of each of their children (one of which is you).

*Does Auntie Ethel look like any of your aunts? I'll bet she has a story to tell that would surprise you.*

*Everyone, no matter how boring you think they may be, has a story to tell. Everyone has little juicy tidbits that surprise others. This is the place to glory in the eccentricities of your relatives!*

*People love to talk about themselves, and people love to talk about others. Gather up information from all the members of your family! It's true that some people can be a little more creative than others, so find them and give them a job! Creative people can often pull creativity out of others as well. It's up to you to make this so much fun that the entire family will want to participate.*

*You may have never met this Gargoyle family, but I'll bet you will go to their web site and read about them anyway!*

⌂ Let's say Ethel (oldest daughter) met Phillip and had five kids (grandkids of the grandparents): Jeff, Robin, Shannon, Cliff, and Topper. Each of the [grand]kids has a link to their own page, showing pictures of their families, bragging about their kids, etc. Each one is a mini family page within the larger family web site.

*This is the rest of Ethel's page. Notice the links to each of the five children. The four oldest kids all have families of their own, and each of their pages has information about all of them.*

*(The News Flash is repeat information from the newsletter, just to make sure the important event is not overlooked.)*

This is Ethel and the adorable children, including the twins, Jeff and Robin, who are as alike as two bookends. To the right are Cliff and Shannon. You can barely see little Tyler Oedipus Philodendron Parenthetical Eudoraman Raspittzel sitting at his mother's feet, but if you click on him you will go to a larger photo of this sweet little guy with the long name, who sings like an angel.

### News Flash!

Entirely out of character, Ethel Frances was arrested recently for mooning the local sheriff. (The reason for this outlandish behaviour has not yet been established, although there are indications that lead one to conclude it has something to do with the sheriff's distaste for Spam, an opinion that Ethel takes personally. Please check the calendar for the date of her court appearance--she'll need some support. Bring Spam.)

Return to beginning of history section

Return to Home Page

# Individual pages

It is entirely up to you how much information you want in your history section. Some members of your family (like yourself, since you're the boss) might like a personal page just for themselves that can give more detailed information, insights, essays, samples of work, etc. Perhaps someone has a small family business—here is a great opportunity to publish that business information on the web, just by including it in the family site. Encourage your relatives to create their own personal pages that can be included in your site. If their page is not actually part of your site, of course you will make links to it anyway, wherever that family member is mentioned. That's the wonderful thing about the web—no matter where the pages are physically located, they are only a mouse click away.

*If you want the information about a business or service to be found by others browsing the web, you need to **register** it with the indexes, which means submitting your URL (the address of your web site) to the indexing services. See the Home Sweet Home Page web site for links.*

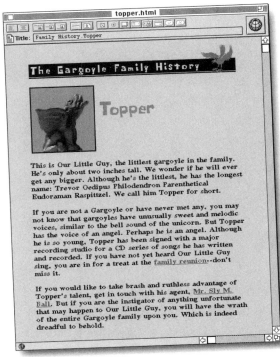

*On this page, Topper has added a link to his agent for potential gigs. Of course, if you sell blue-green algae or edit books or do environmental consulting, you should add a whole page or two of information about your services or products.*

# Linking the pages

After you have created several pages, you are ready to start linking them together. If you haven't already, please read the information about the various kinds of links on pages 113-114. The ones you are ready to do right now are the links that take you from one page to another—from the Home Page to the Family History page, for instance, and from Grandma's page to your page.

Once again, I must recommend you READ THE MANUAL. We cannot give specific directions for every software package available. But it is always a simple process:

⌂ Select the text or the graphic to which you want to apply the link.

⌂ In some applications you will then choose a menu command, something like "Link to...," then choose the page to connect with. Or perhaps you drag an icon from another page to this text or graphic.

⌂ That's it. Easier than you thought, huh?

For instance, in PageMill, this is one way to apply a link:

⌂ Select the text or graphic on the Home Page to which you want to apply the link.

⌂ View the page, let's call it Page Two, that you want to link the Home Page text to.

⌂ See that tiny page icon in the upper left of the window of Page Two, to the left of the word "Title" (shown in the picture to the left of this paragraph)? Drag that tiny icon from Page Two and drop it on top of the selected text on the Home Page.

⌂ Voilà. (You will find more detailed directions for various applications on the Home Sweet Home Page web site.)

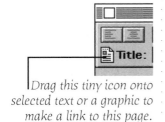

*Drag this tiny icon onto selected text or a graphic to make a link to this page.*

⌂ http://www.peachpit.com/home-sweet-home

# Make it interesting

There is the potential that a family web site could be deadly dull. No matter what you do, most of the information is not going to excite anyone outside of your family. Who cares. You don't want the world poking around in your personal affairs anyway. But the site *should* be interesting to everyone in your family. One way to ensure this is to give family members some inspiration. Send them a list of questions to answer that might pull out unknown tidbits of information. Most people have an easier time answering specific questions than trying to write something general about themselves. Try sending some of these questions to your relatives and see what they come up with. Some of them might surprise you. The wild things Grandma did when she was in her twenties might shock the teenagers in the family. In fact, the wild things *you* did will probably shock your own kids. Good. (Remember, you have the right to edit the work of others.)

You never knew this about me, but . . .

If I didn't have to work for a living I would . . .

If I wasn't doing what I'm doing, I would be a . . .

I love to . . .

I hate to . . .

I love these three things:

I hate these three things:

The wildest thing I have ever done is . . .

The most embarrassing moment in my life was when . . .

–continued

If I could invite any three people to dinner, I would invite . . .
   because . . .

If I could invite anyone in the world to a slumber party,
   I would invite . . .

My favorite movie is . . .

My favorite book is . . .

My favorite author is . . .

My alter ego is . . .

My theme song is . . .

If I could go anywhere back in time, I would go to . . .
   in the year . . . because . . .

If I had been born in 1625, I would probably have been a . . .

When I grow up I want to be . . . (not just a question for kids)

If I had seventeen children I would . . .

There are two kinds of people in the world:
   those who _____ and those who _____.

The quote I live by is . . .

I hope I never . . .

I wish the government would . . .

If I was President, I would do these three things:

The problem with the world today is . . .

I once had a dog/cat who could . . .

And make up lots more!

# Just for kids

If possible, let your children type their own answers directly on the web page. They can, of course, choose as many or as few of these to complete. Ask them to create more questions!

What I like most about being a kid is . . .

I wish grown-ups would . . .

I hate it when adults . . .

I love it when my Mom . . .

I love it when my Dad . . .

I hate it when my Mom . . .

I hate it when my Dad . . .

My favorite person is _____ because . . .

If I were President the first thing I would do is . . .

I hope I never . . .

I wish I didn't have to . . .

My favorite part of life is . . .

I think kissing is . . .

I would rather kiss a dog than . . .   with . . .

The best place to store used gum is . . .

# E-mail addresses

How many people in your family have e-mail addresses? Possibly quite a few. Each time one of your relatives appears on a page, make a link for sending mail to them (page 114). It's okay to be redundant (meaning you will have links to their e-mail in other parts of the web site). In Project 7 (pages 153–156) we'll create a specific e-mail page, but you should also include it whenever someone is mentioned here in the history section so other people can respond to the surprises they will undoubtedly find on the web site.

How can you tell if a link will give you an e-mail form instead of jump you to another page? If you see the "at" symbol (@) in the link, that's your clue it is an e-mail address:

**uncledrag@ugly.com** is an e-mail address.

# Get help

Obviously, your family history section could get enormous. So what. It's cheap. And it's valuable. The only expensive part is the time spent in pulling it all together. But of course you will have help. You need to conscript your relatives into providing information, photos, anecdotes, and what all. The more they can give you on disk, the easier it will be for you. If some of them are interested in making their own web pages, you can divide the work—let each of the individual families make their own personal pages and send them to you for inclusion in the site. Make it a family affair.

# Project Three
# Photo Album

The Family Photo Album section of your web site is a place to post all those great (sometimes embarrassing) photos of family events and gatherings, or individual photos that anyone wants to share with the rest of the family. It's nice to have a little blurb about each photo, with a date and personal note. Perhaps you might want to change the photos weekly or monthly, giving everyone a chance to contribute and to give people a reason for returning to the site again and again. You might have a section of historical photos that never changes, a grandkids section, a babies section, a sisters section, a cousins section, or other groups you have among your family or friends.

Creating games to play with the photos is fun and gets people involved. For younger children, make a list of items to find within the photos. They can e-mail the answers to you and win a simple prize of some sort, like a silly poem or a sound file or some stickers in the mail. For older folks, try a series of what-do-these-people-have-in-common games. For instance, all the photos on the page include a redhead; all the portraits are of people whose middle names start with the letter "R"; all these women gave birth in the month of May; all of these couples have four children; etc. Family members might discover interesting things about each other. They might have to call or e-mail each other to find out what they have in common. This is a great place to subtly involve those family members who do not participate in family events as often as others.

# Photo file size

The important thing to remember here is to make the file sizes of the photographs as small as possible. On a 14.4 modem it can take almost one second per kilobyte to download a graphic image (depending on a variety of variables!), so a 30K photograph may take 20–25 seconds just to display that one image. (For some people it will be faster than this, for others it will be slower.) Imagine if there are 20 photos on the page—no one is going to stick around long enough to see them.

A common technique on web pages is to have a small, thumbnail-sized photo appear on the page, and if the user wants to see a larger image, they can click on the small, thumbnail image and it jumps to another page where the larger image is displayed. The user knows before they open the second page that it will take longer, but that's their choice.

*Click on this image to jump to a separate page that displays the same photo in a much larger size.*

# Thumbnail to full-sized image

To link from a thumbnail to a full-sized image means you must have two completely different files of the photo! See, your web software might let you resize the photo right on the web page, but just because you make it smaller in *inches* does not mean it is smaller in **file size!** No matter how large or small the photo appears on the web page, it is exactly the same file size! This is what the browser is doing:

When you view a page, the HTML code tells the browser what to load. Any graphic images to be displayed are stored in the folder with all the files of the pages you made. When a page that contains a photograph is called upon, the HTML code tells the browser to go to the folder, find the graphic, and display it. If the photograph in the folder is 175K, the computer has to load all 175K worth of information to display the photo, whether the photo is 5 inches wide or 1 inch wide—it's still 175K.

So to use the thumbnail trick, you must have a tiny file of the photograph about 10 or 15K, plus another original, larger photographic image—larger in physical inch size, which will also make it larger in file size. (If you want, you can also make that larger image in a higher **resolution**, which will *really* make the file size big.) On your web page, the smaller image will link to the larger image, which will be on another page, as shown in the example to the left.

In your photo-editing software, resize the images to the sizes you want them on the web pages. For instance, if you plan to display the thumbnail one-inch wide, then resize it to one-inch wide. If you want the thumbnail to link to a larger photo that is six inches wide, make a second version of the photo that is six inches wide.

Before you post a lot of photos, make sure you understand how to create them in the proper format and size—see pages 59–60.

**resolution**: *how clear the image appears to be. Higher resolution means there is more information contained in the image to create the clear details, and thus the file size of the image is larger.*

**Standard resolution for web site images is 72 dpi (dots per inch).**

# Using tables for photos

Most of the web authoring tools have a feature for creating **tables**, which are collections of individual "cells" that let you make columns and rows on a page (did you read pages 115–116 on tables?).

Tables are a great way to display photographs, ensuring the caption stays with the photo. Without a table, if you line photos up across the page, then hit a Return or Enter and type the captions below the photos, there is no guarantee that the person who looks at the page on their own computer will see everything lined up neatly the way you had it positioned. With a table, though, the caption will always be connected to its photo, and the images will not be spread haphazardly all over the page.

*This table has the borders turned off, or set to 0 (zero) (you'll find that command in the same dialog box where you format the table). Without the borders showing, this just looks like nice, neat columns. It's a great way to organize your photo album.*

# Project Four

# The Family Newsletter

Instead of the annual holiday letter that one or two industrious members of the family send out each year, everyone in the entire family can contribute to an ongoing newsletter that keeps everyone in the entire clan updated on exciting (or boring) events all year round. This is a wonderful place to post information about graduations, weddings, divorces, births, hospitalizations, art work from the grandchildren, promotions, and anything else that comes up.

You might want to cajole several family members into becoming regular reporters and columnists. Everyone, of course, is welcome to contribute, but you will probably have more information to post if one or two people feel it is their "job" to gather stories. The older ones and younger ones are most likely to have more time for this job, and it would give them a stronger connection to the project. If possible, have them send electronic files to you. This might be a great way to get Grandma to use her computer more, and to get the kids away from the games and into a word processor, and to get Uncle Lloyd writing once again. Oh, there is so much to do!

# Write stories, not data

Your newsletter will be much more interesting to read and people will keep coming back if the information is more than single lines of data. For instance, don't just state that "Cousin Toomer is getting married to a young woman named FooFoo on April 1." How dull. Tell me more about Cousin Toomer, who are his parents, what has he been doing all his life, where did he meet this delightful French woman, what is her story, what do they have in common, what do they hate about each other already, what are their answers to a few of the questions on pages 125–126, etc. Toomer and FooFoo will feel important and pleased to be written about.

Other family members can be encouraged to send public messages to the Guest Book (pages 170–171) giving Toomer and FooFoo sage advice and explaining lessons they have learned, truths they have discovered, spiritual gifts for the new couple. This serves two purposes: It circulates wisdom throughout the family, since not only can the new couple read the messages, but anyone who goes to the Guest Book can also read them. In addition, when we write from the heart, we bring up wisdom and connections from deep inside of us in a much different way from when we talk. By posting these important messages publicly, all family members will learn more about each other. We will learn things about Uncle Floyd we never knew, we will discover how Grandma felt about being the mother of four children under the age of three, we will be amazed at Ryan's gift of poetry, and so much more. I suggest you find as many ways as possible to get people to write about themselves and their lives, their feelings, their plans, their disappointments. The more we give of ourselves, the deeper and stronger our family becomes, no matter how separate we are physically.

# Story and column ideas

Of course you will have the usual newsletter sort of information on your pages, but you will have more interesting and provocative stuff to read if you assign several family members to regular stories or columns. Or, since everyone is too busy these days, rotate the responsibility of writing a column between three or four people, so each one does a column only once every three or four months. What will they write about? Here are some ideas:

Interviews of the elders by the teenagers

Interviews of the teenagers by the elders

A list of favorite web sites of the month

Stories and artwork from the children

Book, movie, or software reviews

Computer games

Pet stories, pet advice, stupid things the pets in your family do (the columnist can collect stories from everyone)

Pet of the month

Grandchild/Aunt/Uncle/Grandparent/Mom/Dad (etc.) of the month

Travel tips, Health tips, Cooking tips, Sewing tips, Money tips, Business tips, Computer tips, Internet tips, etc. (your family has a wide range of "experts" on many things!)

Cooking tips for bachelors

Handyperson tips (I know the word sounds kind of silly, but I'm a woman and I own more power tools than most guys I know but I just can't call myself a handyman)

Parents-of-Teenagers Support Group

Gossip column

Advice column (à la Ann Landers; someone with a quick wit could make up the letters *and* the answers and have quite a good time doing it)

Bad jokes

Cute Things Our Kids Said (a collection from the family)

Trivia questions (have everyone submit questions, then post a few at a time)

Word and number puzzles

Creative writing, short stories submitted by a variety of family members

Ongoing novel, appearing as a chapter each month; perhaps each month the chapter is written by another family member so it organically evolves in unexpected ways

Genealogy column

Editorials, including guest editorials from the family pets, dead movie stars, past presidents of the United States, angels, etc.

Other newsletter items: want ads, yard sale items before they go on sale in the yard, letters to the editor, current news of the family (of course), and I'm sure you will think of more.

Ask a question each month and have your family e-mail their answers for posting in the next newsletter. Ask questions like those on pages 125–127, or make up more provocative ones. "What is your opinion of the radical right?" "Why should our next President be a woman?"

# Putting it all together

Once you gather the text and illustrations and photographs, you are ready to put it all together on your web site. As usual, you need to make a decision about the format:

⌂ Set all the text on one long page with **anchors** so the reader can jump from story to story.

⌂ Or: create an introductory page with a table of contents that links to other individual pages that each contain a group of related stories and columns.

⌂ Or: create an introductory page with a table of contents that links to the individual stories and columns, with one story on each new page.

⌂ Or: use a combination of the last two suggestions. That is, create some pages that contain a longer story all by itself, and some pages that contain several related stories and columns.

The point is that you should think about the format before you get started (although your decision will probably be made for you contingent upon how much text and graphics you have to work with).

**anchor:** *a link that takes you not to another page, but to somewhere else on the same page. To the user, the underlined text looks exactly the same whether it functions as a link or an anchor. There is no indication that you are going to jump to the same page instead of going to another page altogether. See page 99 for an example.*

⌂ http://www.peachpit.com/home-sweet-home

# The one-page newsletter

If you don't have a great deal of copy, or if you don't have the time to spend to make a big deal out of it, a one-page newsletter will be just fine. As with any long page, you do want to have links (or, technically, anchors) that allow the reader to jump around the page without having to scroll. Here's an example of a one-page newsletter that is simply text, a headline, and a few links. You could do without the fancy headline, of course, but it is so easy to create and the effect is so much more pleasing.

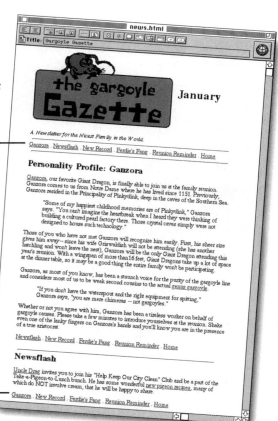

*Notice the line of links across the top of the page. This enables you to pop to any article instantly.*

*Notice that after each story there is the same line of links (minus the link to the current story). Thus anywhere you are on the page, you can always get to any other story or back home with the click of a button.*

http://www.peachpit.com/home-sweet-home

# The multi-page newsletter

If you have been actively soliciting material and have received a substantial amount, you are ready to create a multiple-page newsletter that will really impress your family. You will probably win a very large award.

Make an introductory page, or a "home page" for the newsletter section. On this page, write a little blurb about the newsletter, what it's for, what it means to the family, or what your vision of it is. Of course, solicit volunteers for future editions.

Then make a table of contents. This table of contents, of course, is a list of links that jump the readers to the stories. Links can be set to jump the reader to the top of a new page, or directly to any headline or text or image anywhere else on the whole page. Thus you could have several stories on one page, and the link from the table of contents will take the reader directly to the story even if it is two-thirds of the way down the page.

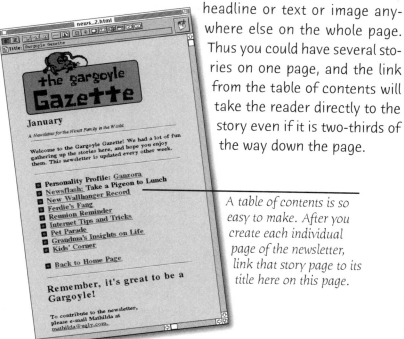

*A table of contents is so easy to make. After you create each individual page of the newsletter, link that story page to its title here on this page.*

# Don't forget the links!

As your readers browse the newsletter, they must be able to jump back to the newsletter introductory page from wherever they are. You might want to add a special **icon** (tiny picture) that readers recognize as the button to click to go back to the table of contents.

Some people, though, are browsing the web with software that does not allow them to see all the beautiful images, which means they cannot see the **icon** as a link. To ensure these people can navigate through your web site, also make a **text** link to the same page. It is not uncommon on the web to see a graphic acting as a link, right above or near the text link that will take you to the very same spot.

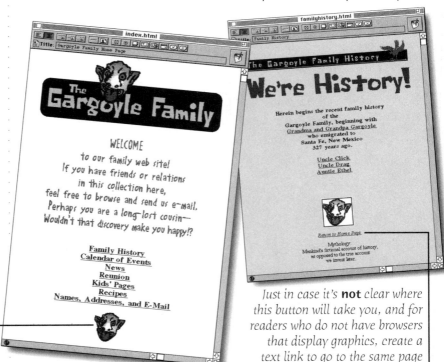

*This icon is pretty easily identified as referring to the Home Page.*

*Just in case it's **not** clear where this button will take you, and for readers who do not have browsers that display graphics, create a text link to go to the same page that the graphic button goes to.*

# Project Five
# Calendar of Events

A calendar of events, combined with a list of important dates, can be a valuable part of your family web site. I, for instance, have a great number of relatives. I don't celebrate the birthdays of each and every one of them, but if I noticed on the family calendar that it was one of my cousin's birthday, I would be happy to dash off a birthday e-mail note. And I would be just as pleased to receive one from any relative. **Just because a message arrives electronically does not make it any less valuable.** Quite frankly, getting an e-mail message from me on a birthday is much more than any cousin has ever gotten before, so our communication and connection has grown significantly stronger.

A calendar of events and important dates announces not just birthdays, though. It can store anniversary dates of weddings, divorces, house-buying events, emigrations/immigrations, bas mitzvahs, bar mitzvahs, christenings, deaths, and more. Celebrate publication dates, graduations, reunions, sobriety, non-marital commitments, holidays both national and obscure, pagan rituals, solstices. It can remind other family members of the date Grandma's plane leaves for Afghanistan, or when Uncle Drag's ship is coming in. Highlight reminders for baby showers, weddings showers, and Cousin Ratcliff's annual bath. Call upon family members for support at court dates, firing squads, PTA meetings, child custody battles, sick bedsides, Christmas caroling, the monthly Sunday Afternoon High Tea, book club meetings, and I'm sure you can think of many more events that people would like to at least know about, even if they can't participate.

*This is the basic groundwork for a typical calendar. By now you know enough to see what is still missing, right?*

*(Did you guess that it needs anchors to jump you around the page and a link to the Home Page? Oh, you are correct.)*

# A calendar with few dates

How you put your calendar together depends on how many dates you have. If you only have a few, say two or three per month, put them on one page and create anchors to each month. Be sure to make anchors that take the reader back to the top of the page so they don't have to scroll up and down (it gets boring). You might want to showcase the current month's events somehow—perhaps make that link larger and bolder, or add a graphic to it.

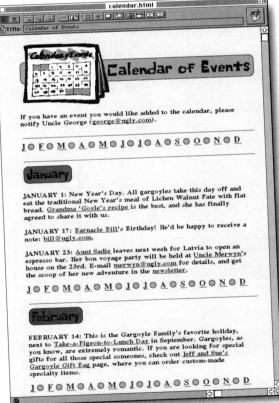

*Since this page is quite long, we added a row of letters that link to each month (J=January, etc.) and copied that row to each monthly segment on this page. No matter where you are on the page, you can instantly jump to any other month.*

*What's missing? Think a minute. :::thinking:::*

*There should also be a link to the Home Page in every monthly segment!*

# A calendar with many dates

If you plan to make each month a full calendar of events, create a separate page for each month. On the main page for the calendar, create links that will jump the user to the separate calendar pages, one at a time. Each of these monthly calendars should, of course, have a link back to the main page. Even better, create links to every other month from each individual calendar (as shown below). This prevents the reader from having to bounce back to the main page constantly. And don't forget the link to the Home Page.

*Above, you see the links to the calendar for each month; each month is a separate page. February is highlighted because it's the current month.*

*Each monthly page, of course, has links to every other month. Links are great.*

# Link important dates

Many of the dates in your calendar have logical links to other areas in your family web site, or perhaps to places outside. For instance, each birthday announcement should have an **e-mail link** to that person so the reader can instantly dash off a birthday wish. Some calendar events are told in more detail within the newsletter, so create a link from the date to the story in the newsletter. Some dates may have relevance to an outside web site. For instance, if Brother Jeff is announcing the date of the Digeridoo Convention where he will be accepting an award, he might want a link to the home page of the Digeridoo Guild.

**e-mail link:** *a link that doesn't jump you to another page, but pops up an e-mail form addressed to that person (see page 114). You just type a subject and your message and hit the Send button.*

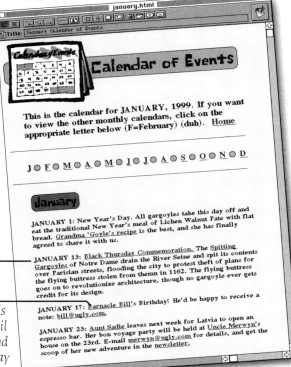

*This is a link to the web site in Paris where this important historical event is reported in great detail.*

*When you click on this link, you get an e-mail form (page 31) to send Barnacle Bill a birthday message. Or any other kind of message.*

# Gathering dates

Of course, as with the rest of your pages, you will need the cooperation of other members of your family or friends to gather the dates. Encourage them to include any sort of date or calendar event they want to share, no matter how silly. If they are *really* silly (thank gawd for silliness), link them to a Silly Page where the event is elaborated. No one can resist playful wit. It is those touches of whimsy that make your web site so delightful and a place where your family and friends *want* to visit regularly.

# Project Six

# Recipes

Your family web site is a wonderful place to publish and share all those great recipes that your family loves. Auntie Lois's potato salad that she brings to every picnic, little Lizzie's unbaked cookies which she is so proud to make all by herself, Uncle Merwyn's famous baked beans, Ryan's broiled sea bass in chard leaves that he makes for every new date, the secret recipe for that incredible cake that Great Grandma always used to make but would never divulge the recipe for that was found stashed in the big Bible after she died, and on and on.

This is a very easy section to create, since it will be mostly text, unless you want to add some graphics or photos. Family members can print the pages right from the screen. This might be a good section to update regularly, another reason for people to return to the site again and again.

Your only logistical decision is whether you want all the recipes on one page, or if you want to make separate pages and link them together. The examples on the following pages show you several options. Note: although this section is about recipes, the concepts of organization and linking are what's important. Similar to the newsletter and calendar, the structure of the pages depends on how much information you have.

# All recipes on one page

**anchor**: *a link that takes you not to another page, but to somewhere else on the same page. To the user, the underlined text looks exactly the same whether it functions as a link or an anchor. There is no indication that you are going to jump to the same page instead of going to another page altogether.*

If you decide to put all your recipes on one page, then you should make links from the top of that page to each individual recipe that appears farther on down. After each recipe there might be links that take you to every other recipe (if there aren't many), and a link that takes you back to the top of the page. It can be very annoying to have to scroll your way up and down a long page.

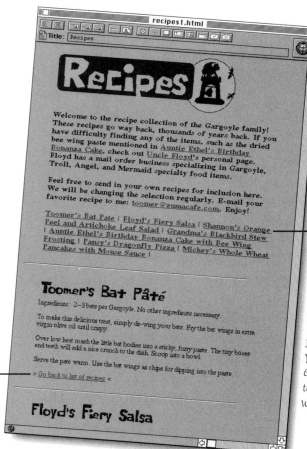

*Each of these underlined recipe titles takes you to that recipe, which is on this same page. The page can be many feet long, so it's your job to make it easy for the reader to move around within it.*

*This link takes you back to the list of recipes at the top of the page.*

# Individual pages of recipes

Another option, rather than putting all the recipes on one page, is to have an introductory page for the collection, with each recipe on its own page. On the introductory page, of course, are links to each of the individual recipe pages. This gives you more room for photos of the food, illustrations you or your children may create, mouth-watering descriptions of the delicious items, serving suggestions, titles of the appropriate music to listen to while making and eating the dish, history of the recipe, folk tales surrounding the food or ingredients, romantic trivia of the dish, etc. Having the recipes on individual pages also makes it easier for readers to print just the ones they want to use.

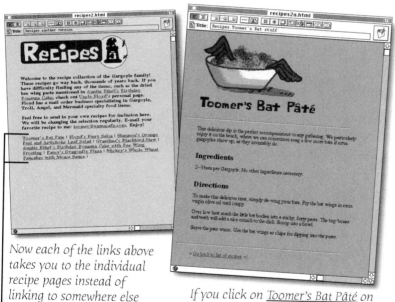

*Now each of the links above takes you to the individual recipe pages instead of linking to somewhere else on the same page.*

*If you click on Toomer's Bat Pâté on the previous web page, you jump to this page. Notice at the bottom of this page is a link that takes you back to the page with the list of recipes.*

*So what if your illustrations of the food items are dorky! Your family (and everyone else) will appreciate them anyway. If you don't feel comfortable making silly drawings, let your children or grandchildren create them. Besides the fact that children are more uninhibited and have that natural charm to their work, they will love the opportunity to be published in color on the Internet.*

# Lots of recipes

If you have many recipes, you might want to group them into categories not only to make the list easier to read, but easier to find what you want. You can make the lists on the first introductory page, with links to the individual recipes, as shown below.

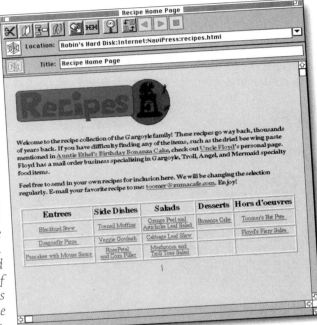

*These categories are grouped using a table (pages 115-116). Each underlined recipe title, of course, takes you to that page with the recipe.*

# Lots and lots of recipes

If you have a *great* many recipes and lots of information, list just the category headings on the first page (as in figure **A** below). Link each of those categories to another page that has a list of the individual recipes in that group (as in figure **B** below). From *that* page, create links to the individual pages (as in the example for Toomer's Bat Pâté on page 149). This might seem like a lot of pages, but the pages are easy and cheap to make, and it's fast to jump from one to the other. If having a couple of extra pages presents the information in a clearer manner, then it's the right thing to do.

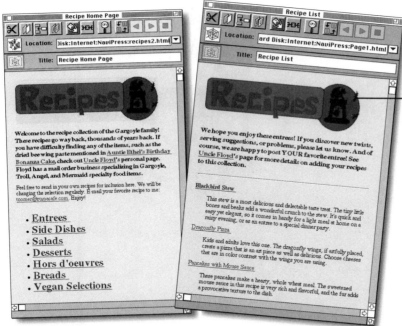

*You can use the same graphic on every page. After the browser has displayed the graphic once, it remembers the image and pours it on the next page very quickly.*

**A**. *Because there are so many recipes in the collection, just the headings are displayed on the first page. Each heading is linked to a listing of the individual recipes (see **B**).*

**B**. *If you click on "Entrees" in **A**, you will jump to this page where you see a list and descriptions of the recipes. Click on a recipe name and you will jump to the page with that recipe.*

# Sharing recipes with other families

You might add links to your recipe pages that jump to a variety of culinary sites on the web. And as other branches of your family build their web sites, you can link to their recipe pages, and they to yours. Or perhaps you have strong Italian lineage in your family, and you run across another Italian family web site with new and exciting Italian food ideas—e-mail them a nice letter and discuss linking your recipes to each other. That is one of the beautiful things about the Internet—being able to share parts of ourselves globally. Take advantage of it.

# Project Seven

# E-Mail & Database

One of the most useful parts of your family web site will be your e-mail page and family **database**. This is a list of every family member's address (physical address at their home), phone number, fax number, mobile phone and beeper if they want them published, and their e-mail address. Several of these people may have their e-mail addresses linked in various other parts of the web site, but having a page devoted to the entire family database makes it so much easier to find someone.

You will set up the e-mail addresses in this list so when a person clicks on it, an e-mail form pops up pre-addressed to that relative. Someone just types in the subject and the message, hits the Send button, and off it goes. Directions for e-mail links are on page 114.

You might want to add other handy information to this database, such as their birthdates, where they work, names of their spouses and children, what kind of cars they drive, their favorite colors, etc. This is meant to be a database, not an entire catalog of their interests and hobbies (that page is elsewhere on the web site), but there is no reason for a database to be impersonal and dull.

**database:** *a collection of lots of pieces of information, or data, nicely organized so you can easily find the piece you want.*

⌂ http://www.peachpit.com/home-sweet-home

# Typing the information

You will, of course, need cooperation in gathering all the information for this page. Some of it you may already have, and some you may have to go looking for. An important thing to remember is to be consistent in your formatting of the items—keep the information in the same order for each person so it is easy to read, skim, and find things. Leave enough space between the names. Perhaps insert a rule (line) between family groups, or between each name and its information. And of course—never type the data in all caps because that makes it too difficult to read.

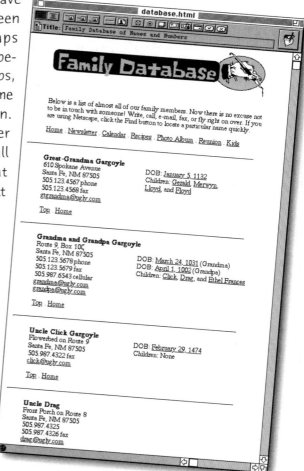

# Finding info on the page

If you are using Netscape (which we recommend), don't forget about the "Find" button at the top of the screen. When you click this button, Netscape asks you what you want to find, and it will search *only on this one page*, **not** everywhere on the World Wide Web. This is handy for searching through a large family database.

*Click on this button to search the current page.*

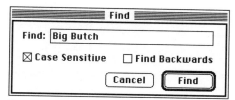

When the Find Box appears, type all or part of the word or words you want to find. You don't need to type the entire name, which can be very helpful if you don't know how to spell it anyway. If you want to find only the words with the same capitalization as you typed, then click in the checkbox "Case Sensitive" ("case" refers to upper- or lowercase). For instance, if you want to find your cousin Blue, but not someone's favorite color blue, then type Blue with a capital B and check the "Case Sensitive" box.

If you have clicked anywhere in the text on the page (anything that wasn't a graphic or a button), you probably left an insertion point flashing. When you click "Find," Netscape finds information from that flashing insertion point and downwards. If you want Netscape to search *above* the flashing insertion point, check the "Find Back-wards" checkbox.

# Sending attached files

Don't forget that with an e-mail message you can also send files as "attachments." You might want to send scans of your kids' artwork, sounds of the baby crying, multimedia love messages to your husband, or any other exciting files you can think of. The rest of the family can send **The Family Webmaster** (that's probably you) updates to the web pages, additions to the database, photos of the pet tarantula, and all other information necessary for the web site. It's too easy.

**The Family Webmaster:** *the person mainly responsible for creating, posting, and updating the family web site.*

*"Webmaster" is a not a gender-specific term— many webmasters are women.*

Either on the e-mail message itself or from a menu, you'll find a button called "Attachments," "Attach file," "Send file," or something similar. Click that button or choose that menu item and your computer will ask you to locate the file. Use the standard procedures to find and select the file through the dialog boxes. Now it is attached and when you send the e-mail message, that attachment will go along with the letter. It will take longer to send the e-mail message when it has a file with it, of course—the larger the file, the longer it will take to send.

Don't forget to compress the file before you send it (see page 52). Some services, such as America Online, will compress the file for you when you send it, but in general you'll have to do it yourself.

# E-mailing everyone

Once you get your database all set up, you and others in your family will probably find times when you want to send an e-mail message to everyone. This is an easy task to do, especially if you are using Netscape. The details may change over time, so check the Home Sweet Home Page website for current step-by-step instructions.

# Project Eight
# The Family Reunion

Many families are spread out across the country, or perhaps even the world. Even if they are all in one region, everyone doesn't have dinner together every night. A family reunion can be a wonderful and memorable event.

Many of you already have family reunions. If you've never had one, it may not be something you are going to start now (although I do heartily encourage it). But I'm sure those of you who do plan, create, arrange, and/or attend a reunion of any sort can imagine how useful a web page could be in the process. You can post the dates, times, schedule of events, and list of attendees as they confirm. You can provide the address and phone numbers of local hotels, with links to the hotel pages (if they have one), and post the best airfares. If people are expected to bring potluck food, make the arrangements on the web page. If you have games planned and need props, make a plea for contributions. If you hired a live band or a photographer, announce it (with links to *their* pages, of course). Oh, this is too much fun.

Even if your only participation is to show up, you could check the web site for a list of hotels and phone numbers in the area of the reunion, confirm dates, jump to links where you can make plane or train reservations, e-mail questions or responses, see the list of other family members who have committed to participating, find out what to bring to the pot luck, and so on.

Since it is so easy to let people know about the arrangements, why not push the event a little further this year. If your reunion is already pretty wild and people love to come and you are excited thinking about it, then okay—you're doin' good. Or if you have a group of people who enjoy simply chatting and catching up with everyone's lives, that is a valuable thing also. But if you think of family reunions as deadly dull, it is your job to spice it up. All it takes is one person to act as the emcee and get people off their behinds. In most groups, this one person has to be creative and dynamic and motivated, because for some reason most people would rather sit on their behinds and be bored. I know this. I have hosted many a large gathering, and one must often force people to have fun. But once you get them up and at 'em, once they are in the game and having fun, once they start laughing, you are guaranteed they are going to go home feeling good and glad they went. Even the real party poopers who refuse to actually join in the games or skits or talent show or sing-along or lip synch end up having just as much fun watching everyone else make fools of themselves. As Zorba the Greek said, "I'm laughing at the thought of you laughing, and that's how laughing never stops in this world."

Oh, but I am getting carried away. I am not here to tell you how to have a delightful family reunion—I'm just supposed to make suggestions for putting together your web page. Okay okay okay.

# Your reunion page

If you have been creating the other pages in this book along the way, you are probably fairly proficient by now in web page design. It's getting pretty easy, isn't it? Just be smart about your links, make a clean page, add some interesting headlines, and your family will be thrilled. You're good.

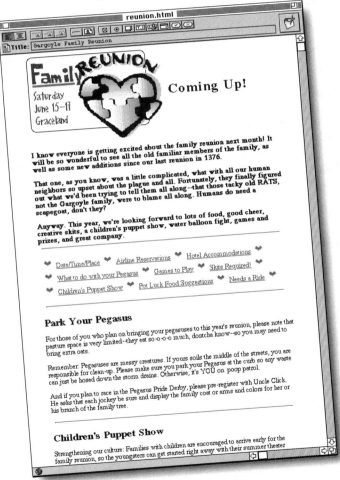

# Other reunions

This chapter could easily apply to high school reunions, or reunions of your Girl Scout or Boy Scout troop, army buddies, fraternity or sorority, writers' group, traveling companions, church, or any other group of people you have bonded to over the years who need a gentle push to come together again. The point, after all, is that we are human. Humans need each other.

# Project Nine

# Special Occasions

Oh, I know you can't wait for the holidays so you can create more web pages! How about a birthday card page, a new home page decorated for the New Year holidays, cards for Groundhog's Day, Mother's Day, Father's Day, celebration cards for the end of school, graduation, winning your insurance lawsuit, publication of a new book, quitting your rotten job, opening a new business, the solstices, a big promotion, William Shakespeare's birthday, and so on.

How about special cards/pages for kids, like "Jack: Hurrah for potty training!" or "Sally: Congratulations on learning to ride a two-wheeler!" or a note from the Tooth Fairy celebrating missing teeth. The Easter Bunny could send children on a treasure hunt, and the family dog can tell holiday folk tales.

These pages should involve the entire family. Everyone can contribute ideas and information, several people can create the pages and send them to you for posting. Even if they don't have computers or Internet connections at home, many towns now have Internet cafes where you can take the kids downtown, get a cup of coffee, pay a small fee, and everybody can log on. A good Internet cafe always has someone to help computer beginners and **newbies.**

**newbie:** *someone new to using the Internet.*

⌂ http://www.peachpit.com/home-sweet-home

# A couple of ideas

By now you know very well how to create the pages and link them.
So use that imagination of yours and surprise someone!

# Updating the files

You (or others) will probably be making and changing these pages regularly. If you want a new page to replace an existing page in your site, **name** and **title** the new file exactly the same as the preceding one. For instance, you might *name* the HTML file as **occasion.html**, and *title* it **Special Occasion Card**. When you "upload" the new version of the page to the web server, the links will still work from existing pages to this one—the new file simply replaces the other file of the same name.

**How do you upload a file?** It depends on your service provider. Call them and ask for specific directions. Usually you can send files to the server from your own computer, but the procedure varies.

Alternatively, you might want to leave the older pages up for a while, and add new pages. New pages will need new links, of course. You might want to make a link from your home page to a new section called something like "It's a Special Occasion!" On the first page of that section, create an annotated list of special occasion cards, with a great big link (like a big button or small graphic) to the most current event. Leaving special pages up for a while makes people happy, especially kids, who can show their friends their own personal announcement on the World Wide Web, long after the event has happened.

*See the information on pages 64–65 regarding the **name** you save the file as, which is different from what you **title** it.*

# Send cards from the web

There are several places on the web where you can create and send a special occasion card directly from a web page. It's really cool. This is the way it might work (details may change): You type in your name and the recipient's name, choose a graphic and some colors or patterns, choose a message or write your own, and click the Send button. The person gets an e-mail message telling them they have a special web page devoted to them, and it tells them the address (the URL). The card stays there about seven days. Some services are free, others charge you.

*The address of these card-sending sites may change, more may be added, some may disappear. So rather than print the current addresses in this book, go to the Home Sweet Home Page web site and just jump from the links we've provided there.*

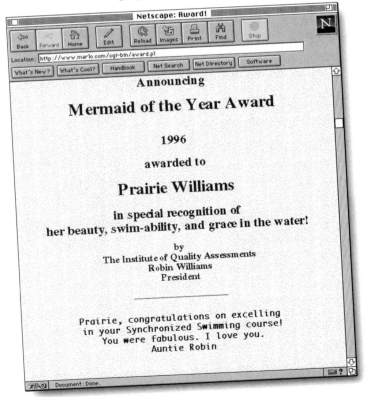

# Project Ten
# Fun Stuff

Haven't had enough fun yet? **Interactivity** on a site is guaranteed to keep bringing people back to your pages. Create some fun games, trivia contests, photo competitions, quizzes, etc. If this is a family site, make up games centered around information about the family, perhaps questions that will require family members to communicate with each other. If this is a site for a group, such as a Boy Scout troop, include games around the focus of the group. This chapter contains several easy-to-implement ideas for adding one more sparkle to your web site.

**interactivity**: *where the reader becomes involved, either by creating something, playing a game, answering questions, downloading information, etc.*

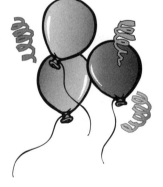

# Ideas for fun pages

These ideas are just jumping off points for you. Once you get on a creative roll, I know more and more ideas will pop into your brilliant mind. Ask around in your family, also—someone just might surprise you with their bent toward silly games.

You could have a question per week, or a list of ten questions per week or month. It's always more satisfying if there is some compensation for winning. Depending on your situation, there might be an actual prize each month donated by family members, such as a cake from Uncle Floyd or a massage from Cousin Willie or a drawing from little Scarlett. Or the prize might be the glory of having your name posted the following week on the web page, along with your correct answers and how you discovered them.

### Family trivia contests

⌂ Make a list of questions about family and events. People may have to communicate with each other to discover the answer. For instance: Who has a middle initial that starts with Q? Who graduated from college in 1942? Which mother in our family hitchhiked across America when she was 18 years old? Where was Great Grandma Weber born? Which family members have tattoos? You get the idea.

### Search the Web

⌂ Create questions that require people to search the family web site for answers, or perhaps even to search the entire web itself. If there are people in your family who are new to the Internet, this might give them an opportunity to practice their research skills. Along the way, they will become more adept and at home with this oh-so-important communication tool (with helpful tips from you, of course).

## Stories

⌂ Start a story online. Write perhaps two or three exciting paragraphs, then leave it hanging. Appoint someone else to write the next few paragraphs, and post their addition. Someone else writes the next few, and so on. Just keep posting the chapters as people write them. Make no plans, no agreements on outcomes or situations or problems or characters. Let the story evolve.

⌂ A variation of this is to write the first couple of paragraphs. Someone writes the next few paragraphs, *but you only post the last sentence*. The next person continues the story based on that last sentence. Each time, you only post the last line of the next contribution, and the next person builds on that. After you have several pages, or the story evolves to some sort of completion, post the entire collective story. It's guaranteed to be a riot.

## Name That Tune

⌂ If you're comfortable posting sounds (see the Advanced Projects chapter, page 170), put up little sound clips of well-known songs for an online Name That Tune game.

⌂ Name That Relative. Just who is it disguising his voice to sound like Inspector Clouseau?

⌂ A variation on this is the radio game Name That Sound. Record things like the sound a popsicle wrapper makes when you pull it off the popsicle; your dog yawning; a razor sliding over a dry, rough beard; one of the grandchildren crying; any number of interesting sounds that would be hard to identify out of context.

### Coloring contest

⌂ This family web page below is, obviously, a coloring contest. Kids (or adults) can simply print the page (in Netscape, just click the Print button at the top of the screen). Then they can color it in and send it to some ambitious family member (you) who can scan the finished drawings and post them back on the web site.

Check the Home Sweet Home Page web site for links to places on the web where kids can color directly on a web page!

# Advanced Projects

There is so much more you can do to your web site, but more advanced projects need more advanced skills than this book can provide. Plus the software changes so often, and everything gets easier and easier. The laborious steps you take today for some of these projects may be completely unnecessary in six months. Check out the Home Sweet Home Page web site for more details and how-to information on some of these topics.

Here are a few suggestions you may want to think about. You can always hire someone to do these for you right now, if you really want them. Ask your ISP (Internet service provider), or ask at your local Internet cafe.

## Make your web site private

⌂ It is possible to set up your web site so only people who know the password can gain access. It's not that difficult to do—you just need to find someone to write the **script** for it.

**script**: *complex code that tells the computer to do something, like collect information from a form and send it to an e-mail address.*

## Add video clips

⌂ Before you can add a video clip, you need to make it. It's not very difficult to do it, but you do need special software and hardware and knowledge. You can hire someone to take your home videos and make clips for you that you can post. It's a worthy investment, I think—what a treat for the grandparents to see videos of the grandkids!

## Add sounds

⌂ Sounds are actually one of the easier advanced projects to accomplish. What a treasure for Auntie Shannon on the east coast to hear Little Trevor on the west coast wish her a special happy birthday message! You just need a couple of **helper apps** and some knowledge—knowledge about how to make the sound file in the first place (which can be as easy as talking into the microphone that came with your Macintosh), converting it, attaching it to your web site, and playing it.

*helper apps: small applications that help you do things on web pages (see page 61). The Home Sweet Home Page web site has links to many helper apps for your advanced projects.*

## Have a guest book

⌂ I love guest books. You may have seen some sites that have them (like the Home Sweet Home Page site)—they usually say something like, "Sign our guest book!" Then there is a space where you type in a message and it gets posted to the web page for everyone to see. Anyone else coming to that site can post a note in response. What a great thing for a family site! But it takes some specialized scripting. Again, you can hire someone to do it for you.

## Providing files for downloading

⌂ You may want to have photos, a text file of information, or other files available for family members to download—they just click on a button and the file transfers to their computer. This is not very difficult to achieve. Talk to your service provider.

It is even easier to attach a sound file, a graphic, a scanned image, etc., to your e-mail and send it directly to friends or family members. First you have to make the file, then simply send it as an attachment. Your e-mail software has a menu item somewhere with the option to "Attach file," "Send file," or something similar.

# Review of the Process

The process of creating a web site, as you have discovered, is a very organic, living, exciting process. There are a lot of steps between the idea and the completion. These steps are scattered throughout the book, but here is an orderly list of the pages where each of the concepts is explained. Most of the items don't need to be followed in this specific order; for instance, you can certainly create the map before you get the software.

| | |
|---|---|
| p.58 | Acquire the web authoring software. |
| pp.63–68 | Read Chapter 5 so when you start creating pages you will know how to name and organize them. |
| pp.76–78 | Decide what will be on your family web site. You can always add to it as you go along. Make a map. |
| pp.82–83 | Write the text. Save the text as ASCII (or make Mac clipping files from SimpleText, as explained on the web site) |
| pp.84,88,90 | Create the graphics. |
| p.60 | Save the graphics in GIF or JPEG format. |

pp.85–100    Read Chapter 9 about basic web page design.

pp.107–111   Create your Home Page.
             Name and title it properly.
             Put the text and graphics on it.

p.112        Create another page in your family web site.

p.113        Link the two pages together.

             Make some more pages.
             Add appropriate links and anchors. pp.113–115
             Use tables when necessary.  pp.115–116

pp.72, 113   When you are finished, test your links and make
             sure your graphics show up.

pp.66–68     Check again that the files are organized properly.

pp.70–72     Take or send the files to the web server.

p.163        Update files when necessary.

# In Grand Conclusion

There are two important characteristics of well-designed web pages that keep people coming back over and over again to the same sites: **new information** and **interactivity** (letting the reader become involved in some way). Don't let your site become static. Parts of it will stay the same, of course, such as the family database (except for new addresses and numbers), but much of it can and should be changed quite often. As I've said before, try to get as many people in your family or group of friends involved as possible. That's part of the point of this entire project—**the process is as important as the product**. Involve your kids, your Grandma, the cousin who is rather reclusive, the black sheep of the family. Buy Grandma a computer and a connection, if you must. I guarantee you will be amazed by the results. And you will have fun.

If you have some great ideas you would love to share, please go to the Home Sweet Home Page web site and send them to us! We will post them, along with credit to you. If you develop a family/friends web site you are proud of, let us know the address and we will link from Home Sweet Home Page to your site. Because when it comes right down to it, we are all one family.

# A Quick Peek at HTML

Odds are you'll create all of your HTML (hypertext markup language) documents using a graphical editor like Adobe PageMill. That's just fine. On the other hand, there may be times when you want to make some small adjustments to your web page that go beyond what's handled by your web authoring software.

An HTML document is nothing more than a bunch of text marked up with a series of **HTML tags**. You can get extremely complex with the design and layout on your page using these tags, but the basic code is fairly straightforward. This section does not pretend to teach you how to write HTML, but is provided simply to 1) show you what you did not have to do to create your site, and 2) give you a peek at what you can expect should you choose to go beyond the basics of your web authoring software.

http://www.peachpit.com/home-sweet-home

Here's an example:

```
<HTML>
<HEAD>
<TITLE>This is the title of the web page</TITLE>
</HEAD>
<BODY>
Here's some text for my web page. I think I'll put a paragraph tag here
to tell the web browser to start a new paragraph.
<P>
This text will appear as a new paragraph. Now how about adding a
horizontal rule, to provide a dividing line between this text and the
next chunk of text.
<HR>
This text is the final text in the HTML file.
</BODY>
</HTML>
```

Notice all the angle brackets (< and >) scattered throughout this text. Each pair of angle brackets encloses an **HTML tag**. Each tag has a different meaning. For example, <HTML> denotes the beginning of an HTML document.

Tags frequently (though not always) occur in pairs. Add a slash( / ) to the **start tag**, put it at the end, and it becomes an **end tag**. For example <TITLE> marks the start of the title of your HTML document and </TITLE> marks the end of the title.

Certain tags are frequently used alone. For example, the **horizontal rule tag** (<HR>) inserts a horizontal line, used to separate different areas of your web page. The **paragraph tag** (<P>) tells the browser to start a new paragraph, starting with the next block of text.

The illustration below shows how the Netscape browser displays the HTML code from the preceding page. Note that the title of the page matches the title we specified. Notice the horizontal rule?

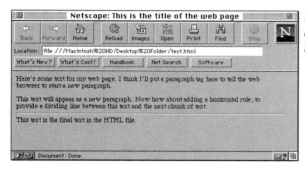

*Here's how the HTML code is interpreted by a web browser.*

The URL of the above document starts with the word **file**:// instead of the more usual **http**://. That's because I opened an HTML file on my hard disk instead of opening one on the web. As you design your own pages, open them using your web browser to verify that they look right before you send them over to your web server.

(By the way, the "%20" that occurs in the URL shown in the Location field in Netscape stands for the space character. Spaces in a URL are generally considered a bad thing, and Netscape uses the secret code %20 instead. Everywhere you see %20, just think space.)

There are a lot of HTML tags to master if you want to write directly in HTML instead of using web authoring software. If you're interested in learning more, pick up a good HTML book and start reading. Check out *Learn HTML on the Macintosh* by David Lawrence, or *HTML for the World Wide Web: Visual QuickStart Guide,* by Elizabeth Castro. You can see a sample chapter of the *QuickStart Guide* in the Past Picks section of the Peachpit Press web site (http://www.peachpit.com).

# ᴥ *Index*

**in which you find what you hope to find**

## Colophon

This book was created in
PageMaker 6.0.1 on a
Macintosh. The typeface for
the body copy, headlines, and
subheads is the Humana Sans
family from ITC, with some
Humana Serif Italic thrown in.
The typeface for the chapter
openers is Blackadder, also from
ITC. The great swashes you see
in Blackadder are alternate
characters in the font.

The sample web pages were
created in Adobe PageMill,
Adobe SiteMill, NaviSoft
NaviPress, or Netscape
Navigator Atlas Gold Beta.

The photos for the sample web
pages and for Robin's picture on
the back cover were taken with
a Kodak DC40 digital camera.

Browser Dawg and Url Ratz
were conceived by Robin
Williams, Scarlett Williams,
Harrah Argentine, and Ronni
Madrid. Their delightful
illustrations were created by
John Tollett. They are trade-
marks of Ballyhoo.Inc.

# About the Authors

1/97

## Robin Williams

I live and work in Santa Fe, New Mexico, one of the most beautiful places I have ever seen. I'm a single mom of three great kids. I write a lot of books. I teach. I own an Internet cafe here in Santa Fe called Zuma's Electronic C@fe, where we feed people and teach them how to connect and what to do once they get there. I'm excited to be part of the history of the Internet—it's as great as being on a wagon train.

### Other books by Robin Williams:

*The Little Mac Book*

*The Mac is not a typewriter*

*BEYOND The Mac is not a typewriter*

*The PC is not a typewriter*

*Peachpit's PageMaker 5 Companion*

*Jargon, an informal dictionary of computer terms* (with Steve Cummings)

*Tabs and Indents on the Macintosh*

*How to Boss Your Fonts Around*

*The Non-Designer's Design Book*

*A Blip in the continuum*

## Dave Mark

I live in Arlington, Virginia, with my wife Deneen and our son Daniel. We are expecting a new little one any day now! I'm a partner in Zuma's Electronic C@fe, and I share Robin's enthusiasm for things Internet. The Internet is a tremendous enabler, bringing us much closer together in this global village.

### Other books by Dave Mark:

*Learn C on the Macintosh*

*Learn C++ on the Macintosh*

*Learn C++ on the PC*

*Learn HTML on the Macintosh* (with David Lawrence)

*Learn Java on the Macintosh* (with Barry Boone)

*Macintosh C Programming Primer, Volumes 1 and 2*

*Macintosh Pascal Programming Primer*

*Mac Programming FAQs* (with Steve Baker)

*Ultimate Mac Programming*

http://www.**peachpit**.com

http://www.peachpit.com/**home-sweet-home**

http://www.peachpit.com/peachpit/meetus/authors/**robin.williams**.html

http://www.spiderworks.com/**dmark**

http://www.**zumacafe**.com